Wild & Wise Witch

Wild & Wise Witch

DAILY MEDITATIONS
TO OPEN YOUR PATH

Terri Clifton & Bev Adamo

Published by Wild & Wise Women

Cover art by Richard Clifton

Book design and cover layout by Crystal Heidel

Paperback ISBN: 978-1-7338118-3-5
Hardcover ISBN: 978-1-7338118-5-9
EBook ISBN: 978-1-7338118-4-2

www.wildandwisewomen.com

Dedication

To our moms, Norma and Joan, without whom we would not have been as Wise or as Wild. And all the women of our lineage, names lost to time, who lived and loved and learned before us.

We wrote this with the hope of bringing the courage and strength of our foremothers through to these challenging times. May it be a spark for any woman willing to claim her unique presence, power, and abilities.

ACKNOWLEDGMENTS

Gratitude beyond words to the early supporters of this book so many thanks to Patrice, Denise, Paula, Susan, Diana, Alise and all the women who traveled through the year of *Wild and Wise Witch* along with us:

Jean Kathryn Carlson, Alchemistical Dream Master

Chiara Adamo, Daughter Extraordinaire

We would also like to thank the men in our lives who not only accept, but strongly advocate for their wild and wise women.

INTRODUCTION

The path of the Wild and Wise Witch is a journey of authenticity and reconnection. It is an invitation to rediscover your senses and expand your intuition. You will fund your own energy, choosing when and how to use it. In pursuit of magic you will recognize and follow your own rhythms as you observe the seasons, cycles, and patterns all around and within you. Intention, focus, energy, and action will become working tools. You will recognize that magic is everywhere, and yours begins in you.

This book is here to help you get out of your own way. To inspire deep knowing and trust in yourself, so that body, mind, and spirit work in tandem for your highest good. Each day you'll find a thought or two to work with and consider, simple rituals, bits of knowledge. It is by no means meant to be comprehensive on any single subject, but rather cause consideration of each. Let it make you curious and seek to learn more.

This journey goes within, taking you through the body/mind/spirit as a system. It begins by seeking the magic in every day. It begins with knowing yourself so deeply you come home to yourself, and the rhythm and pulse of your existence. Magic is something you already are. Knowledge and experience can be gained. Empowerment is an inside job. Living with intent and authenticity is power. Using your vision, dreams, and will is craft.

Use this book as a tool in your own way. As a daily source of inspiration by following the calendar or as an oracle, opening randomly for a bit of knowledge or insight. It is as simple as beginning. May it lead you along your personal path and illuminate your magical possibilities. You are limitless. Believe in yourself and you will be unstoppable.

The Winter Witch

The Winter Witch is full of wishes, imagination, dreams, love, and hidden gifts. She is a being of fire and ice, light, and dark. She is whole and holy, embraces the clarity of the night sky and knows her deepest self. She marvels at the infinite uniqueness of the snowflakes and of herself. Through the dark season she carries her own light and warmth, and dares to imagine a life of audacious authenticity, discernment, intuition, and personal power. The Winter Witch is the wisest of the season sisters, holding her own council and space.

Embrace and Celebrate
Winter Magic

- Spend time beside a fire, or Yule log.
- Read a book set during winter.
- Write a story, poem, or memory.
- Try winter foods from around the world.
- Listen to beautiful music.
- Look for joy and remember to play.
- Make kindness your gift to others.
- Listen to your own voice.
- Make wishes.

Symbols, Scents, & Such

Pine, Mistletoe, Holly, Oak

Frankincense, Myrrh, Cinnamon

Rosemary, Peppermint

Candles, Lanterns

Stars, Moon, Sun

Ice and Snow

December

December brings the longest night and celebrations of light all around the world. It is a time of comfort, joy, and peace as well as wishes and magical moments. It also begins the going-within time, when nature draws down, trees and animals change their rhythms and adapt. This beginning of the winter season is for keeping close to the fire, a time for stories and dreaming. Reflect and come home to yourself, listening to your own voice in the stillness.

December 1

Magic is natural. You knew this when you were young. Conditioning, environment, fear of what others might think are all things that can separate us from our true selves and by extension our magic. Play, curiosity, and openness are a few things that reconnect us. Remember, you are older now and you can choose a magical life. No awpproval or experience needed. You have full permission to be you. Follow your joy.

**Light a candle and visualize
your own path opening.**

December 2

*Agency is your very own power, your ability,
to affect the future.* — *Albert Bandura*

Sounds like magic, doesn't it? A sense of control in the challenges and situations of living, in your abilities to both survive and thrive. You can choose to influence your own thoughts and behaviors and trust you can handle all that comes your way. It is both stabilizing and adaptive. Create or expand your ability to access your power of choice. Make excellent choices for yourself. The power is yours.

**Claim your agency and abilities
to affect the future.**

December 3

Authenticity is essential for reaching the full potential of one's personal power. The more real you can be with yourself the more information you have to set intention and use energy effectively for making your magic. Audacious Authenticity is a lifestyle of finding and embracing, and then living from your whole and sacred Self. It allows us to live and love and learn without restriction.

**Where in yourself do you hide
your uniqueness and confidence?
What would it look like to embody
your truest Self?**

December 4

Your body is made of chemicals and electricity, stardust and minerals. Your senses translate the outside world for your body as information becomes an actual energy current that races to your brain. This creates emotions, thoughts, and memories. Increasing awareness of the state of your body enhances intuition and self-choice. A body that is ignored can become unbalanced, unhealthy, and uncommunicative. The brain is your interface between body and magic.

**Give your body what it requires
to think clearly.**

December 5

Energy can't be created or destroyed, only transmuted. Magic requires energy. The more you can generate, the more you have to work with. You can experience exhaustion in all aspects of life. Increase or decrease the energy by the choices you make in your physical, mental, and spiritual life. Notice what makes you feel good. Pay attention to anything that drains you. Adjust accordingly.

Meditate on drawing clear energy into yourself, restoring and healing. Relax and hold onto it like sitting in the sun.

December 6

Intention is what you want to happen. It is directed impulse, a powerful tool for setting and achieving goals. It is the arming and aiming of your will and is fundamental to using magic and manifestation. You can just let life happen to you. Or you can consciously engage with yourself. Listen to your own inner voice. What is it saying? What do you need? What do you want? There is power in knowing.

**Go outside. Breathe. Find a
place you can talk to yourself.
Ask questions.**

December 7

Focus is a point of directed concentration. It is not only attention, but the application of will.

Practices like mindfulness, meditation, and visualization can help train your brain to increase focus and calm distraction. A healthy brain that is nourished, stimulated, and rested is more capable of holding concentrated effort. Notice when you do and do not feel your focus is strong. Begin to train yourself to increase attention and concentration. Make it fun.

Learn a language, practice brain training games, or play a musical instrument to enhance focus.

December 8

Your actions tell the universe how serious you are about your intentions. Action in Magic is taking your longings and desires into the physical world. Your words, movements, and directed consciousness are brought to bear along with the tools of focus, intention, and energy. Without action power stays dormant.

Are you serving yourself well with the actions you take? Are they leading you where you want to go?

December 9

Biological rhythms are natural cycles of change in chemistry and functions in the body. Beyond ourselves we can see cycles everywhere, from day and night to tides and seasons, to the earth's orbit and beyond, and yet we forget we are nature. Give attention to what your body is doing. Learn your moods and reactions. Discover where you carry your stress, or sense danger. Pay attention to the changes in yourself, your own seasons and tides.

The better you are at picking up your own physical signals the more you can trust your intuition.

December 10

The moon has spoken to something inside us since ancient times. Art, literature, music, and myth repeat the lure of the moon. We watch the steady phases of the dark moon to full moon and back. Learn which one speaks to you but watch for the beauty of each. To shine at night has always been a magical thing. Embrace the cycle, let yourself notice, drawing or releasing as you need. Flow.

Glow. Grow and let go.

Remember you are both shine and shadow.

December 11

Daily routines done with attention and intention are simple and powerful rituals. Stirring your tea, washing your hair, the possibilities are endless for inserting your personal practices. Light a candle, soak in a bath, and call in your best self. Those small seeming things take you back to your innate Magic. Discover it. Only you can.

Love yourself, discover yourself, and choose yourself. This is how you embody your craft.

December 12

If winter is your favorite season, embrace it. Make it a celebration of your favorite things. If you find winter difficult and long, consider viewing it as an opportunity to practice staying present. Instead of fighting and losing a battle against a season, get to know it. There are lessons and gifts. Challenge yourself to find small things to enjoy every day.

Life is lived every moment. None are unimportant. Don't wait to be Magic.

December 13

Wise women have always been seekers of knowledge, and lifelong learners. It is never too late to pick up a new skill or learn about something that calls you. Use the dark quiet of winter to begin to transform. Read stories that teach, or ones that transport you to imaginary worlds. Take a class doing something that your curious inner child still gets excited about. The brain learns faster when at play.

A Wild and Wise Witch sees no difference between learning and playing.

December 14

Comfort as self-care goes well with long nights. Creating a soothing atmosphere with fire, candles, or twinkle lights can change the energy of our surroundings and lower our stress. Nature is resting. Seeking the soft and warm puts you in sync with the season and works a subtle magic on our spirit. Allow the peace of the season to reach you.

Whenever you see beautiful lights let the warmth seep inside you and fill you with calm, comfort, and love.

December 15

Music is as old as humanity and has been part of ritual since the time of cave painting. Babies are born with sensitivity to rhythm and tone. It is a magic all its own that can be used with intention. Combined with breath or movement it can reset the body and the mind. Try it for focus, healing work, creativity, or an instant change in energy.

Create a playlist to help manifest a goal or heal. Follow your instincts and create the energy you want to match.

December 16

Nyx is the goddess of night, one who emerged from the primordial chaos, and was feared even by Zeus. She is often depicted with dark wings or riding a chariot, trailing stars. Winter is her season. Female and shadow, and powerful. Women have been taught to hide both their strength and their darkness. Consider what inside you may be a strength or a depth you've been shamed from. Reclaim it.

**Visualize walking out of chaos,
leaving a trail of stars.**

December 17

Memories are made from moments. Being present in your own life puts you in the only place you have any control, the now. Winter scenes, scents, tastes, sounds, and textures can all become practices in being alive to the moment. Joy in the depth of winter comes from the simple and the beautiful. Our best memories are from times we are truly present.

Stay alive to simple joys and fragile beauties. Let your heart be open to seeing them everywhere.

December 18

The days are almost at their shortest in the northern hemisphere. Deciduous trees have withdrawn their sap, their leaves have released, and are no longer serving. Can you identify what no longer serves you? What can you release and not carry with you throughout the rest of winter? The trees trust that new growth will come in time. Do you?

Notice the bare trees and the changed environment. Sense the cycle all around you. You are part of it.

December 19

Discernment is the ability to see things as they really are and to make wise use of what you find. Choices, changes, relationships, boundaries, and integrity of self are all served when see and act with clarity. Practice discernment to strengthen your skill. Remove your emotions and observe your world. Are you making conscious decisions, or only reacting?

Visualize a beautiful crystal ball that shows you the truth. Look at anything you want.

December 20

Helya's night falls in the season of Yule. Rituals invoked ancestral energy and the divine feminine, blessings were spoken over sleeping children, and vigil was kept by the fire through the night. The 8th century historian Bede noted that it coincided with Christmas Eve, and unsurprisingly became overlaid by Christianity and equated with Mother Mary.

**Light a candle and hold space for
the women who bore your line.
Write down as many of their
names as you know.**

December 21

The Winter Solstice for the northern hemisphere occurs the instant the North Pole points farthest away from the sun. This point of time and space occurs for everyone on the planet simultaneously. Humans have observed this solstice since the Stone Age. Stonehenge is aligned to its sunset. Newgrange in Ireland and Maeshowe in Scotland are aligned to its sunrise.

**Watch a sunset or sunrise to
mark the longest night and the
return of the sun.**

December 22

Winter celebrations of light and the return of the sun occur in cultures all around the world. Yule, Saturnalia, Shab-e Yalda, Soyal, and many more. Feasting, fire, singing and dancing, traditional storytelling, and vigils are held through the night.

What associations do you have with the celebrations of Light?

**Create your own celebration
of the season. Decorate with
greenery or cook special foods.
Play music or write a poem.**

December 23

The North is often considered the spiritual direction of winter, and Polaris is considered to be the North Star. It is the direction of mystery, reasoning, and introspection. Its element is earth, grounding for the body, letting the mind open. Wisdom is found in the silent night. Be aware of your own internal North Star, the center of your intuition and sacred communication.

**Stand outside on a clear night.
Locate the North Star. Ask for
whatever guidance you seek.**

December 24

Christmas Eve is a night of children's wishes, but perhaps the child in you still exists. Wishing is a magic nearly everyone does at some point. Birthday candles, coins in fountains, and falling stars are just a few ways of wishing. We all have wishes inside us. Some of our wishes sit deep and remain unspoken for a long time. Invite yourself to consider that this is the right time, your time, to focus on what you want. What do you wish for?

Winter is for Deep Magic and Wild Wishes.

December 25

Peace can exist without perfection. It can be invited in even as we suffer turmoil. The search for peace can seem in vain if we only look outside ourselves. Only after taking root inside our hearts and minds can the change be created in the outer world. Search yourself for fears, resentments, and anger. Decide what you can change, accept, or release.

Visualize a heavy snowfall. Each flake brings compassion and love. Breathe and watch it fall, covering everything.

December 26

Bells are used by many religions and practitioners of magic across the ages. They are associated with the element of Air. A multipurpose tool in magic it can be used to summon or banish, seal intentions, cast circles and set spells. Ringing a bell releases energy in sound waves. Scientists have learned to use sound for levitation of particles, generation of electricity, and even brain surgery.

Use a small bell as a pocket charm. Ring it to reduce stress or invoke your power.

December 27

In a society that pushes itself to the edge on a regular basis you must understand that rest is crucial. Resting the body keeps you healthier, promotes clear thinking and helps create a positive attitude and mood. More energy is available both mentally and physically. You can't feel empowered when you are exhausted. Make rest a priority and your body will repay you. Grant yourself permission to sleep and wish yourself sweet dreams.

Evening rituals help create better sleep rhythms. Things to try include warm beverages, soft lighting, aromatherapy, and meditation.

December 28

Making a cup of tea is a simple and easy way to practice ritual. Your choices should represent your intentions. The tea itself can be soothing or energizing. The cup can be bright and fresh, include writing, have belonged to your grandmother, or handmade by an artsy friend, as long as it has meaning for you. Stir in your intention. In the casting of spells clockwise is the direction of increase and healing.

Any time you stir a beverage you can focus on an intention or mantra.

December 29

Reading books opens whole new worlds of knowledge and understanding. Our minds expand, as do our possibilities. It has been shown to lengthen lifespans, lower stress, and increase empathy. There have been times in history when it was dangerous for a woman to know how to read or own a book as it was associated with witchcraft. Many were tortured and put to death.

**Be a dangerous, magical rebel
for knowledge and literacy.**

December 30

Shadow work can sound intimidating when approached with superstition, but without our shadow we aren't channeling wholeness. Not every moment or emotion will be light. We all experience the heavier side of life, and ourselves. Learning to sit with the uncomfortable and discovering ways to clear it removes triggered responses, granting you the chance to respond rather than react. It can be your superpower.

Shadow is not an enemy. It is part of you, and it looks out for you. Shadow survives.

December 31

The old year is almost gone. The new one is nearly here. At any crossroads of time or place we can stop and choose direction, move forward consciously, so we must be present to what is, who we are, and why we are doing the things we do. Commit to making conscious decisions in the coming year that serve you and your values.

Instead of resolutions, try a list. Write your top five priorities. Do your current choices align?

January

January brings a New Year and wide open possibilities going forward. The cold and the dark bring opportunities for unseen transformation. Deep in winter, January's energy brings stillness, introspection, and quiet aspiration. Consider what possibilities exist within you. Deep winter is for wild dreaming. Listen to your dreams, and nurture them with attention and knowledge, but work in silence. Stay within your dream space and hold the vision. Protect your dreams. There will be time later to share.

January 1

The past is behind you and can't be changed. The future can be what you make of it but much depends on the choices you make in the Now. If you had the power to make your dreams come true, what would that look like? What habits, knowledge and tools would it take to embody that life? Imagine achieving them, then work backward, noting the steps it took. How did you get there? Now make a map.

Mantra for January: I will create my future.

January 2

The more clearly you can visualize what you want the better chance you have of attaining it. Planners and vision boards are two ways to begin making dreams and goals visible and tangible. Words and images focus your mind and your magic, keeping your path clear.

Use a planner for the year. Fill in important dates. Think about what you want from each month. Add touches of personality. Create space for the words in your head. Write lists, track your choices and actions, and reflect on whether they match your intentions.

January 3

Strengthening your senses will provide your mind and body with better information to work with. In the coming weeks let yourself become more sensual and sensitive. Experience your world. Use your senses with purpose. Tune in to your surroundings. Practice builds strength. Sensory practice can aid with staying present, and with reducing anxiety.

Let your senses teach you about Winter, with all the sights, scents, and tastes. Listen. Feel. Learn.

January 4

Dance has always been part of ritual, seduction, celebration, and art. We humans have danced since the beginning and all over the globe. Children will dance to music before they can walk. It is born in us, but we often lose that openness and connection as we age. When did you stop dancing? In rediscovering yourself, you invite the chance to connect to one of the physical tools of magic, movement.

Dance is a simple addition to any ritual or manifestation ceremony. Add music that matches your energy, and just move. Let your body speak. No rules.

January 5

Trusting yourself means believing in your abilities, decisions, and intuition. With confidence in yourself, you are more likely to take risks, pursue your dreams, and achieve your desires. Build more by setting small, achievable goals, practicing self-care, and surrounding yourself with supportive people. Communicate with yourself.

**Challenge negative self-talk and
habits and replace them with
positive affirmations and actions.**

January 6

Candles have an ancient history of ceremony and ritual, though their origin is unknown. Egyptians believed a candle near a sleeping person brought dreams and divination. In modern magic and craft they are used to focus intention. Combined with color, spoken or written words, the cycles of moon or seasonal changes, they are a component of spells, ceremony, and manifestation.

Personalize your candle magic. Don't worry about rules. Making your own combinations is creating your Magic.

January 7

Kitchen witchery attracts those with a love of cooking and homemaking. Canning peaches or making bread may not look like brewing potions, but stir in blessings, love, and intention, and it is magic. A wooden spoon is a wand in the right hand. The hearth was once a special place, the heart of the home. Hearth craft is witchery that revolves around home and family.

Make kitchen magic. Cook a meal or bake a treat. As you combine ingredients, season, chop or stir, add gratitude, protection, and love.

January 8

It is natural to quiet down and retreat into comfort during deep winter. Nesting and creating areas of comfort and quiet joy can bring mental warmth that feels luxurious and helps combat seasonal melancholy. What brings you comfort? What quiet activities do you enjoy?

Create a nest for yourself. It can be a comfy chair with a reading light or a blanket fort or even a dedicated room. Make it a stress-free zone where you enjoy books or movies and a cup of something delicious. No work!

January 9

Janus, the namesake of January, was a Roman god with two faces. He represents duality and beginnings and corresponds to doorways, thresholds, and gates. What passages are you making or considering in your life? Are you seeking a beginning, an ending, or both? What do you need for the transition?

Place a small key on a chain or a ribbon. Use it as a touchstone to commit to and bring energy for the change you seek.

January 10

The words you think, say, and hear all hold power. Different parts of your brain activate depending on whether those words are positive or negative. Learning to really hear what is sounding in your head is powerful, because then you can correct or direct energy to your greatest good. Your brain is a powerful tool for your magic, if you learn to work with it and train it.

Write a single word on an index card representing something you want to increase in your life. Put it where you see it daily. Say it aloud.

January 11

Science is still discovering new and important aspects of human touch, and they already know it relieves pain, helps preemies gain weight, reduces cortisol, and lowers blood pressure. Healers have known this forever. Massage stimulates the sense of touch, opens you to receive and perceive, and is one of the oldest forms of medicine.

Find a partner, a professional massage therapist, or teach yourself how to perform personal massage and get into your own skin. Know your whole self.

January 12

Dream witches revel in the mysterious, imaginative, and visionary, and follow their own path. They may use dream journals, practice divination, use herbs, celebrate moon rituals, or grow night gardens. The intuition of the Dream Witch is strong and sensitive, and she often seeks solitude to balance herself. Dream magic is found in many cultures and has various practices and mythology. Lucid dreaming is controlling and interacting with the dream.

Experiment with seeding your dreams. Write down what you'd like to dream or an answer you seek. Place it under your pillow. Meditate before sleeping.

January 13

Everything humans have ever made, including every bridge or building, started with a dream, a vision, an imagining. Allowing the daydreams and listening to the nightdreams are how the vision becomes the tangible. Magic is conscious change, transformation on purpose, working will. It has driven men to success for centuries and is called genius or ambition. Only in women does it cause fear and become witchcraft.

What dreams are inside you?

January 14

Animals find what works best for them in winter. Some use color to blend in the landscape such as the arctic fox, polar bear, or snow leopard. Others, from the bumblebee queens to grizzly bears, hibernate. Still others migrate thousands of miles. It is a matter of survival and making it through to spring.

Imagine yourself as an animal in winter. What are you? How do you spend the season? What are your strengths?

January 15

Alchemy was a forerunner of chemical science. Once seen as absurd for their search for the Philosopher's Stone, modern scholars are only beginning to understand the depth of alchemists' contributions to medicine, metal working and fundamental chemistry. They explored the natural world looking for its hidden nature. Alchemy is the power of transformation, creating change and transmutation, power that you as the alchemist can use.

All science began as magic.

January 16

Conscious nourishment, or mindful eating, can improve absorption of nutrients from food. Even when eating less healthy food, we absorb more nutrition if we enjoy the flavor, relax and savor, and limit any distractions. Tapping into the mind-body connection and being present and conscious in its care has benefits for health and magic every day.

Visualize the nourishment in foods absorbing into your body. Notice how you feel.

January 17

Each of us, whether we attune to them or not, have a set of core values that are reflected in our priorities. How we choose to spend our time and energy, and how we care for ourselves and others, are decisions based on that core. It is hard to ground ourselves when we lose touch with that center or when we are not living in accordance with our beliefs. Even when we cannot immediately affect our situation we can begin to know ourselves better, and make small but important shifts needed for change.

What are your core values and does your life currently align with them?

January 18

Solitude is being alone without being lonely. The conscious act of spending quality time with yourself is an opportunity to develop a deep inner richness. While loneliness is depleting, solitude renews. It builds creativity, empathy, and self-knowledge. Give yourself some time and space to simply be. Listen. Breathe.

Pictish witches were traditionally solitary, and many magical practitioners across time and place preferred to work alone.

January 19

In Greek mythology Selene was the personification of the moon. She brought the gift of sleep that allows for dreams, and even visited dreamers to bring answers they sought. Unlike other goddesses with temples, Selene was worshiped in the sky.

Lunar eclipses were once blamed on witches who called down Selene with magic and spells.

Crystals associated with the moon include selenite, moonstone, clear quartz, opal and diamond.

January 20

Every snowflake that falls is perfectly individual, with its own special beauty. And every person that breathes life is just as distinct. In a world that is trying to make you conform, claiming your uniqueness is a superpower. The better you know yourself, the easier it is to do. Lose the fear of being different. Embrace it. You are a perfect snowflake.

What do you bring to the world that no one else can? How do your gifts and perspectives serve you?

January 21

Conscious and wakeful daydreaming can reshape your reality. You can heighten your awareness and focus, while at the same time always allow for the creative and imaginative. This is where solutions and innovation often come from. What feels like rationality can be narrowing possibility through fear or conditioning. Think bigger. You have it in you to make things happen once you dream them up.

Flow with the dream. Will the knowledge, skills, and opportunities to show up when you are ready to use them.

January 22

Ebbs in energy are normal. The energy output of our brain and body isn't constant. Downswings can be opportunities to pause our ambitions and brainstorming, let the body rest. But the mind can benefit from low-stakes creativity. Simple coloring can decrease body ache, sleep, anxiety and more. It activates the frontal lobe which involves organizing and problem solving.

Sketch, doodle or draw. Gift yourself crayons or markers and a coloring book of images you enjoy.

January 23

We use our will in the world every day. Most of the time the choices are small, and we barely give them thought. I want, or I don't want. Applying our magic is just a slight shift. Intention, focus, energy, action. Once you know what outcome you seek you can apply skills and tools to make that happen.

Notice your choices both consciously and passively. Are you truly choosing what you want? Will you make the shift?

January 24

Getting what you need is often a matter of allowing it. Time, energy, or abundance are not served with a perspective of lack. While there are numerous magical means to approach gaining what is wanted, the simplest is learning to hold the vision. When you allow the dream to slip, momentum can go with it. Even when you feel stalled or face obstacles, know that is part of the journey. Do not quit too soon.

Release distraction and lack.
Hold the vision.

January 25

Under the bed or under the stairs? Where did your Monster live when you were young? During this time when there is more darkness than light, gather your courage and be willing to look under your bed or stairs or inside your thoughts. There truly are doubts and demons and disparaging thoughts. Invite each of them out into light and watch how many of them simply evaporate because you are willing to look them in the eye. Some doubts may actually hold clues to epiphanies and new freedoms.

**Doubts and demons disappear when
you bring them into the light and
see the truth of what they are.**

January 26

Ancient Greek philosophy held that all things were comprised of four elements – earth, air, fire, and water. Various practices from Druidism to Wicca use these correspondences to focus or enhance magical workings, and the twelve signs of the zodiac are grouped by them.

Reacquaint yourself with the elements. Walk barefoot on the earth, practice conscious breathing, ritually bathe, or light a candle. Which element resonates?

January 27

Barriers offer protection, but they also keep out experiences and emotions that enrich our lives. Boundaries are healthy limits and standards we place around ourselves, decisions about what is acceptable. They allow for growth to occur and new knowledge to be gained. They protect but do not constrict.

Caim is a Scots Gaelic word for a circle of protection and sanctuary. Visualize protection then cast by hand or walk a circle.

January 28

You are the most important person in your life. Loving yourself and taking care of yourself first isn't selfish - it's necessary. When you prioritize your own well-being, you have more to offer others and can show up as your best self. Give yourself the love and care you deserve. You'll be amazed at how much more you have to give to the world.

Begin to nourish a passionate love affair with yourself and your life.

January 29

Paleoanthropologist Genevieve von Petzinger studied cave art all over the world and discovered that in addition to painting animals, early humans were using signs that are consistent across continents and time. She theorizes an early system of communication predating Sumerian Cuneiform by thousands of years.

If you had to write your wisdom to others in symbols, what would that look like?

January 30

The celebration of the Hindu goddess Saraswati falls around the end of January with a festival preparing for the arrival of spring. Depicted with four arms, she holds a book, a rosary, a water pot, and a veena. She is a goddess of knowledge, language, music, and the arts. She symbolizes creative energy and power in all its forms, including longing and love. Her color is yellow.

Seek new knowledge or make some art. Celebrate the mind-spirit connection.

January 31

The Celtic Queen of Winter and goddess of cold and winds, the Cailleach determines how severe the season is, and how long it lasts. Each year on February 1st she needs to resupply her firewood. If she wants winter to last, she makes it sunny and bright for the gathering. If it is gray and cloudy, she is sleeping in, and Spring will come sooner. In Irish myth the Cailleach could transform into a wolf. She is a protector of deer.

**Set or reset your intentions for
the remainder of winter.**

February

February begins winter's transition into spring. It can bring a restless energy, a stirring of all that lives beneath the snow, wondering when it will be time to awaken. It is a time to consider what lessons and plans you will carry with you into the next season and nourish them. There is promise ahead. Turn your face to the light. This last month of the winter brings the chance to celebrate all things love and call more of it into your life.

February 1

Imbolc is a cross-quarter day falling mid-way between winter solstice and spring equinox. Celebrating the rising of the light and spring's return, it is sacred to the Goddess Brigid, a Celtic goddess of inner fire, spring, poetry and fertility. She was later syncretized with the saint of the same name. The energy of Imbolc is both gentle and fierce. It is hopeful and resilient.

Light a white candle at sunset.
Feel your inner fire.

February 2

The first stirrings of bulbs and seeds are working underground, beginning to emerge naturally toward the light above ground. Lengthening of the days becomes noticeable. The next weeks will bring subtle but real feelings of change. What inside you is stirring and needs your attention? What is waiting to awake and reach for the light?

Be still and feel for signs of opening and growth. Allow the process.

February 3

Love Magic is allowing and increasing the energy of love in and around you. Compassion, along with the willingness to be vulnerable and care openly, affects health, relationships, and our purpose. Daring to love this life, the people, and the planet, is brave, courageous, and much needed right now.

Dare to love life. Let it love you back.

February 4

The Sensual Witch is a romantic soul. Passionate and highly sensory, she is emotionally intuitive. Charming and sociable she loves celebrations and events where she can shine, but also enjoys intimate tete-a-tetes. Love spells, charms and enchantments are her specialty. Her magic may include glamour, poetry, potions, and floral essences. She is a creator of pleasure.

**Write a self-love poem or indulge
in a scented oil massage.**

February 5

Passion is defined as strong emotion or inclination. Passionate enthusiasm heightens energy, focus, and willpower. When combined with action and discernment it can lead to fulfillment or purpose. When maladjusted it is the fuel behind anger issues and poor choices.

**In passionate situations ask
what serves your greatest good
and check in with your intuition
before using your power.**

February 6

The oldest discovered jewelry was found in a Moroccan cave. Thirty-three beads made from sea snail shells dated to 150 thousand years ago from the Aterian Culture. Jewelry is and was a form of social information, and communication of wealth, skills, or status within the community. Magical uses include protection and manifestation, glamour, focus, spells, and divination.

Choose a piece of jewelry to remind you of your magic.

February 7

Fire is used magically to cleanse, protect, or invoke. Correspondences are the direction South, and colors of fire such as crimson, gold, orange, and copper. Wands and athame may also be used. Pyromancy is divination by fire, either from gazing into the flames alone or adding various ingredients. Spices such as cinnamon, pepper, turmeric or ginger can represent the fire element.

Carry or wear a carnelian or garnet as a fire charm.

February 8

Rumination is a thought process disorder where the thinker repeats negative thoughts and experiences, or even neutral thoughts in an overly analytical way. Such patterns cause anxiety, depression and illness. They can become dangerous and are rarely productive. Meditation and journaling are tools for managing thoughts and focus.

Ritual release of negative thoughts might involve a workout to music followed by herbal smudging and a shower.

February 9

The first known references of crystal use come from the Sumerians who used them to make magical formulas. Crystals and gems were also used by the Egyptians, Aztecs, Romans, Greeks and all around the world for magical, ceremonial and healing purposes. Chinese and Indian Ayurvedic medicine have used them for thousands of years. Crystals as talismans and jewelry date to the stone age.

Explore gems and crystals that resonate for you, considering color, texture, and vibe.

February 10

If you have been training your senses individually now is the time to challenge yourself to cross train. Visualize color while giving or receiving massage. Let a piece of chocolate melt on your tongue while listening to music. Begin to stretch your sensory abilities. Possibilities are nearly endless. Enjoy the play.

Identify your strongest and weakest sensory skills. Practice them while staying present.

February 11

All your emotions are valid. Not all of them are true. When we are tired, stressed, ill or in pain our emotional responses can distort our discernment and our responses to stimuli. We can be hyperreactive or go numb. Persistent negative emotions can cause body wide inflammation and trigger disease. Consistent positive emotions are healthful and energizing.

Note how your body and your energy react to emotion. Practice a pause between trigger and response. Honor your feelings by sitting with them honestly, but don't let them rule you.

February 12

Glamoury is the craft of control and projection of personal physical energy. It tweaks the perception of the observer. Whether you wish to draw attention or become unnoticeable, glamour can help you get where you want to go. Begin to consider how you wish to be seen, or not. How you move, speak, dress, adorn yourself, your posture, your diction, and your energy all affect what you emanate.

I claim and control the energy I project. No one else defines me.

February 13

Conjuring love comes in many forms. Written words, charms, philters, rituals, potions, amulets, dolls, and singing are some of them. The oldest written erotic love spells are in cuneiform on tablets found in modern day Iraq. Modern spells stress self-development rather than subjugation of someone's will. The aim is to increase self-love to the level that becomes magnetic and attractive.

Attract, don't chase.

February 14

There are theories but St. Valentine's story isn't clearly known. Geoffrey Chaucer wrote a poem about 1380 saying "For this was on Saint Valentine's Day, when every bird comes there to choose his mate" and it became a Lover's Day. The oldest known Valentine (1412) was from the Duke of Orleans, imprisoned and wounded in the Tower of London, to his wife. Make it a day to celebrate love for self and for others.

Attract and send the energy of love in a simple ritual. Pink candles, crystals or flowering herbs are some ingredients used in love invocation.

February 15

Sixth century coins depict a silphium stalk on one side and a heart shaped seed pod on the other. A species of giant fennel, it resisted cultivation but grew wild in Cyrene and contributed to the economy. It had many medicinal uses but became so popular as a contraceptive that it was gathered into extinction. It became a symbol of love and lovemaking that continues to have meaning today. Recently a Turkish scientist claimed to have rediscovered the plant and its medical possibilities are being studied.

The heart shape of the pods may have led to the use of the heart shape in romantic love.

February 16

Smell is the only sense directly connected to the limbic system which processes emotion and memory. Scent is an unseen power that sends messages through the air affecting body, mind, and spirit. Magical sources of scent can include oils, incense, candles and burning herbs. Divination spells, healing rituals and glamour magic all use scent and the bodily reaction to smell.

**Choose a personal scent that evokes
the energy you want to project.**

February 17

Mirrors have been used for summoning, protection, projection, scrying, and divination. They can be used for glamour and beauty spells, and for calling the self to the self. The oldest manufactured mirrors were found in modern day Turkey. Made of obsidian and with a convex surface eight thousand years ago, their polished surface reflects well.

When you pass a mirror, look into your own eyes. Use the moment to connect with the spirit behind them.

February 18

Amulets ward against sickness, evil or hexes. Over time they have existed in the form of relics, herbs and stones in small bags, rings, written spells and burial jewelry. Talismans are intended to bring luck, power, and positive energy. Made often from crystals, gemstones, or metal they can bear inscriptions as well.

Create talismans and amulets using your own instincts and associations unique to you.

February 19

Aglaonice, an ancient Greek astronomer who could accurately predict eclipses, was considered a sorceress for her ability to draw down the moon. The Wiccan ritual performed by a priestess and invoking the Triple Goddess is an indirect reference to her work. She and other female astronomers associated with her from the 3rd to 1st centuries were called Witches of Thessaly, a region steeped in magical lore of all kinds.

Design your own rituals for working with the phases of the moon.

February 20

Lockets as jewelry descended from containers for protection amulets. Written words, small objects, hair, herbs, or ash might be placed inside. A bespelled locket might be used as a pendulum for divination. Not just pendants, lockets were worn on bracelets and rings. Other forms of container jewelry include prayer scrolls, wish boxes, and poison rings.

**Container jewelry can be
used with almost any spell.
Use your imagination.**

February 21

Khione was the Greek goddess of snow, daughter of Boreas, god of the north wind and Orithyia, goddess of cold mountain winds. Often depicted with long white hair and blue eyes, she drives a chariot pulled by white horses or a sled pulled by white bears. Unlike other winter deities her influence extends to spring when she becomes the Lady of Flowers bringing warmth and melting the snow.

Be a Goddess of your own transition as you move into spring.

February 22

Life is full of obstacles and walls that can feel like dead ends. Learn to look for the door - it may be hidden or disguised, but it's there. And if you can't find a door, create one. Visualize breaking down the wall brick by brick or climbing over it. And there are always practical, "right now" steps. Seek support, learn new skills, or use a different approach. Engage your wisdom and stay wild. You got this!

I have the power to overcome obstacles and succeed.

February 23

Divination has been globally practiced for millennia. Pendulums, cards, writing, runes, I Ching, dowsing, spirit boards, tea leaves, scrying, palmistry, and even induced trance states are among the many methods. It has variously been used to attempt to discover hidden or obscure meanings in events, choose direction for undertakings, and for personal fortune telling. You can even do something as simple as flipping a coin.

**The Universe is always open to
support you in your life. You just
have to ask. Listen. Act. Make it
one of your daily Rituals.**

February 24

The end of winter comes with the thaw. The increasing angle of sunlight eats away at the ice and snow. The great sleep is coming to an end. Search out the places within you that feel frozen over. What we don't release stays and hardens. Nothing new can grow until you shine light. Gently, drop by drop, let what no longer serves you become liquid, transform into water for renewal.

Place ice in a dish on a sunny windowsill. While it melts, practice breath and release.

February 25

Sigils are symbols designed and used for ritual magic since the Neolithic era. In the Middle Ages they were associated with alchemy, angels and demons. Modern witchcraft still employs sigils created to amplify intentions and manifest. Corporate logos are a form of sigil, and many include hidden meanings.

> **To create your own sigils, start with clear intentions of what you want and be creative. Sigils can be carved, written, drawn on the skin, or worn as jewelry.**

February 26

The Ouroboros is an ancient symbol that depicts a snake or dragon swallowing its own tail. It is most often interpreted as a symbol of eternal cycles of birth, death, and rebirth. The image occurs worldwide including Norse, Indian, Egyptian and Greek cultures. It was adopted as a symbol by Gnosticism, Hermeticism and Alchemy for unity of all things and perpetual change.

The universe and everything in it is in a constant state of creation and destruction. Recreate yourself as necessary.

February 27

As we journey through life, it's easy to fall into patterns and routines that bring comfort and control. It's important to remember the value of remaining curious and open-minded, no matter our age or circumstances. That way we're constantly seeking out new experiences, perspectives, and knowledge. This can lead us to discover hidden talents, passions, and opportunities we may have never known existed.

Cultivate curiosity to expand possibility.

February 28

Charisma comes from the Greek word Charis meaning "gift of grace." It is the ability to attract or influence people. While it can seem to be a mysterious quality it is possible to become more charismatic. Develop your confidence. Move and act with purpose. Be interesting. Charisma is beyond beauty, it is the power to fascinate.

**Developing skills of glamour
magic can increase your
confidence and magnetism.
Practice projecting your energy.**

February 29

Even the best intentioned and conscious life includes course adjustments. Be aware which of your intentions could use an adjustment, where your life may be off course. Be unabashedly honest. Allow yourself to bring something new into your intentions. What are you so drawn to be or do? Especially, deliciously, what terrifies you to become or do? Set your new intention and then leap. Jump. Run to meet your future self now.

**What would your life journey be
if you chose to live this day, every
day? To name and leap toward
your desires every day?**

The Spring Witch

The Spring Witch is ready to grow and bloom. Emerging from the dark and cold into warmth and light, she embodies her own possibilities. She knows growth requires nourishment and gives herself what she needs. She revels in the freshness and the renewal. Her senses are open, and she embraces and trusts new beginnings. She uses water, fire, earth, and air to connect to the rebirth in and around her. The Spring Witch is both tender and vital. She is the brave sister, trusting the growth that allows her magic to blossom.

Embrace and Celebrate
Spring Magic

- Read Poetry about Spring.
- Splash in a puddle or dance in the rain.
- Connect to the east and the dawn.
- Have a tea party.
- Decorate eggs.
- Spot the first flower.
- Clean your spaces.
- Fly a kite.
- Stretch and move.
- Plant something.

Symbols, Scents, & Such

Cherry, Jasmine, or White tea

Chives, Elderflower, Mint, Lavender, Rosemary, Thyme, Lilac

Eggs, Rabbits, Birds

Flowers

Potions, Tonics, Oils

March

March is transitional and unsettled, a clash of cold and warm that can be very stormy. Rain alternates with tender, bright sunlight to bring renewal and rebirth. Animals emerge, move from survival into thriving as life blooms again. The Vernal Equinox occurs this month, bringing equal day and night before the days lengthen to summer Solstice. March brings the opportunity to consider your own regeneration and renewal. Let the March winds carry away what no longer serves. Allow Spring to cleanse your life.

March 1

Meteorological Spring brings possibilities to lie before you in the lengthening days. What do you want for yourself in this season of growth? How do you need to nourish yourself to support your intentions? Embrace these weeks of early waking, the last of winter overlapping. It is time to stretch and ease into new beginnings.

**Light a candle and sit quietly.
Invite the essence of spring
inside yourself. Let it fill you
with hope and energy.**

March 2

Emerge and look around. Nature is waking from the sleepy darkness of winter and so are you. What lingers from the dreams of winter? Are there longings within you that you ignore or postpone? The time has arrived to bring them gently into the light.

Visualize waking from a deep sleep. Imagine stretching your body, and then opening any blockages you have in pursuing your magic. Give yourself permission.

March 3

Pay attention to signs of your innate rhythms and what draws you to develop your own rituals. What is your favorite time of day? Your favorite seasonal food or activity? Sunshine or rain? Go in the direction that feels most like you and embrace it, but also develop it and add to it. You are still becoming.

Every breath I take is a prayer.
Every move I make casts a spell.

March 4

Bulbs are beginning to get the signals of light and warmth. Under the soil they are starting to reach for the sky. Long before they spread their blooms and beauty, they are stirring. Let yourself be called toward your own becoming. Quietly reach for your inner self. Nurture and protect what you find there. Allow the light to reach you. Let it wake you.

Take a walk. Note the angle of the sunlight and the length of shadows. Notice any plants showing new growth.

March 5

What are you planting in your life? What do you want to grow? Nature grows on its own. Gardens must be cultivated. Your life will progress, but if you want it to produce specific things, you must plant them, tend the soil, water, and remove the weeds. What you get out of it will depend on what you put in, and what you remove to allow for growth. Nurture yourself and tend the garden of your life.

You are the gardener of your days.

March 6

Once you dream the dream you must hold the vision. It is easy to wish and to want. Dreaming is free and effortless, but once you have discovered what it is you want you must be ready to do the work. One of the most difficult parts of manifesting is holding the vision. Belief in yourself cannot be replaced with any other tool or skill.

Is what you want worth the effort? If the answer is yes, Do Not Give Up. Focus.

March 7

The trees are forever challenged by the wind, but it is also how they dance. With no resistance trees cannot build resilience and will fall over as they grow taller. Learn to bend without breaking. Gain strength through overcoming challenges. Trust your roots to hold you. When the winds come, sway.

Dancing with the wind is an act of transformation, and a source of energy.

March 8

International Women's Day is a global celebration of women's achievements and a focus on the challenges still faced every day, all over the world. Take today as an opportunity to both learn about the past and affect the future. Read a woman's story, have a meaningful discussion with friends, visit a museum, or lay flowers on a grave.

Light a candle to the Divine Feminine and call in empowerment for women everywhere.

March 9

In the landscape the old year's remains are revealed with the snow melt. The relentlessness of the wind finishes off the old grasses and leftover leaves, breaking them down, making way for an explosion of new growth. Take the lessons of the last year and let them be compost for your dreams. Make way for new and wonderful things.

**Stand in the wind and cleanse.
Let the withered and worn in
you blow away. Breathe and hold
space for the new.**

March 10

Have you thought about the difference between intuition and instinct? An instinct is usually born from the lizard brain working with the creative intelligence of your body and its cells, to push you in a direction that will serve you. The thinking mind is not usually engaged except as an afterthought of following your instinct. Intuition can be defined as a message from whatever you determine as your Source. More than a feeling, it invites our thinking mind to participate as we choose how we will use our intuition.

Befriend and embrace your intuition and your instinct allowing both to guide you.

March 11

The first flowers of spring are both delicate and hardy. They can be tiny but spread across a hillside or meadow they can be stunning en masse. Often the first signs of change are very small and unheralded. Train yourself to look for the onset of both internal and external transformation. This puts you ahead of the curve and prepared to adjust accordingly.

Begin to give attention to small details and notice how they telegraph coming events.

March 12

Herbal tonics are solutions of herbs or plants for nourishing and invigorating the body. In the spring many cultures gathered the first green plants such as dandelion, rhubarb and ramps for steeping. Roots and barks would be decocted. The resulting liquids contained nutrients, antioxidants, anti-inflammatory compounds, antibiotic, or antiseptic properties meant to restore vigor after winter deprivation. What does your spring body need? What does it crave?

Take steps to jumpstart your spring energy with self-care.

March 13

The Oracle of Delphi, also known as Pythia, was a diviner and prophetess in Greece. Tradition says the oracle first belonged to Gaea, the Mother Goddess, but was stolen or given to Apollo. The Delphic priestess was usually over 50, lived apart from family and dressed as a maiden. Chewing bay leaves or breathing vapors triggered a trance. Her prophecies were recorded by priests.

**Above the Oracle chamber
were the words, "Know Thyself",
which is considered to be the
beginning of all Wisdom.**

March 14

Incantation bowls, also known as magic or demon bowls, are simple pottery bowls with words painted or inscribed. Often personalized, they were a protective form of magic. Those written in Jewish Aramaic or Mandaic included scriptural quotes or rabbinic texts. Christian bowls were written in Syriac.

Inscribe your own spell or wish inside a bowl. Use upon an altar to hold small magical items. Can also be buried.

March 15

Plants growing wild or on a windowsill will attract the Green Witch. Her love of herbs and flowers and trees may result in a thriving garden or a shelf of homemade tinctures. She often feels most connected to her magic and intuition while spending time in nature and feels grounded with her bare feet touching earth. Green Witches tend to bring calm everywhere they go.

Take a walk in nature with your senses open. Hug a tree. Plant a garden or learn about wildcrafting herbs.

March 16

The word Awen is loosely translated to mean inspiration or essence of being and is symbolized by three points and rays of light. In Welsh myth it is the inspiration of the bards and poets and is associated with the story of Taliesin. A person who is filled with the inspiration and flow of Awen is called an awenydd.

When creating, especially writing or music, visualize the light of Awen filling you head to toe. Open to receive your muse.

March 17

When you deal with overwhelm, become exhausted or anxious, grounding yourself is a useful practice. Literally connecting with the earth or visualizing it can each lower cortisol, increase blood flow, and help clear panic and pain from the body. Return to nature to balance and recharge. Use your experiences of calm connection in meditations and self-care spells.

Where do you connect with the earth best? What in nature calls to your soul? Develop your own rituals of grounding.

March 18

The sacred feminine was worshiped among many early societies in the form of the Mother Goddess. Her various names included Gaea, Mut, Cybele, Inanna and Ninhursag. For the first 200,000 years of human existence, long before religions were established, art and ritual represented a female creator.

The divine feminine is alive in you. You carry ancient magic in your blood and bones. The Mother Goddess is both a nurturer and a warrior. So are you.

March 19

Potions are liquids made as medicine, poison, or spells. In the Middle Ages healthcare was often only available from the village wise woman, though very few women could practice medicine. Potions were bought from apothecaries, midwives, courtesans, and enchanters. A love potion is called a philter. In modern craft potions are used for health and beauty, healing, or in preparation for ritual or divination.

Make a simple potion with herbs or teas, add honey or intentions to taste.

March 20

Persian New Year falls on the first day of spring and the celebration includes a deep cleaning of everything in and around the home. Khaneh Tekani translates as "shaking down the house." Clearing your own spaces opens new flow in your life so declutter, scrub, toss, and invite the energy of freshness into your home.

Once cleaned, add scent to your home in the form of flowers, incense, candles, or oils. Bless your space.

March 21

The Equinoxes occur when the axis of the earth tilts neither toward nor away from the sun, which sits directly over the equator creating roughly equal day and night twice a year in spring and fall. Ostara celebrates the vernal, or spring, equinox and is named for Eostre, goddess of the radiant dawn. Celebrations of renewal and birth are symbolized with eggs, birds and flowers. Easter's date is determined by spring's equinox and the moon phase.

**Create your own celebration
for equinox.**

March 22

In increments the days will grow longer. Let yourself embrace the strengthening light. Lean into the lengthening days. As the power of the sunlight grows, receive it as energy for creation. Spring is an excellent time to set physical goals or begin projects that create or build. What have you been waiting to begin? Now may be the time.

**Spring mantra: I have the power
to create the life I want, and like
the sun I grow in power daily.**

March 23

Spring is a time of renewal and life. With flowers blooming and birds chirping, we are reminded of the beauty and the power of transformation. It prompts us to let go of old habits, patterns, and negative energy, and welcome new beginnings. Do not let the past decide your future. Every day is a chance to be reborn.

Embrace the beauty and magic of spring as it unfolds and know that this includes you. Celebrate Spring! Celebrate you!

March 24

We save things in our being, sometimes without recognizing the amount we have collected. It's impossible to fill your life with what you desire when it's full of thoughts, beliefs, people, places, patterns of behavior and things that no longer serve you. It's time to take your life back and prioritize your well-being. Good things are ahead. Make room.

Where in your body, mind, or spirit do you need to clear space for abundance and happiness?

March 25

Your actions and your words matter. Everything you do affects the wider world. When you embrace and strengthen your personal power it is important to remember this. We are co-creators with life. We plant seeds of intent with our words and send out waves with our actions. Not all the outcomes can be known, but it is wise to consider the possibilities.

Responsible use of power avoids causing harm. Self-knowledge and core discipline are key components.

March 26

Humanity is the essence of compassion, the love and kindness that exists within every individual. It's the ability to empathize, to understand and offer comfort. Falling in love with humanity means embodying these qualities and recognizing the value of connection and interaction. Embrace your sacred humanness.

Whether it's through acts of kindness, volunteering, or having empathy towards those around you, there are endless ways to demonstrate your love for humanity.

March 27

Frustration over situations and limitations uses our energy and can be exhausting. That same energy can be redirected for use and benefit our higher good. Next right action can be as small as doing the dishes. Baby steps give us the chance to strengthen ourselves in body, mind, and spirit, making us ready for what is already trying to reach us. Small positive actions break through limitations.

Prepare the way for what you need and want in the future by strengthening yourself in the now.

March 28

Flowers, whether fresh or dried, made into oils or incense, worn on the body or placed within sacred space, are used in magical practices around the world. When creating your own magic with flowers consider your personal associations and experiences. What memories or individuals do you associate with their smells? What color appeals to you, or triggers emotion?

Choose a flower that represents you in some fashion and incorporate it into your magic practice as scent or symbol.

March 29

You are capable of achieving greatness and turning your darkest moments into victories. When you feel helpless, hopeless, and in despair, know that within you lies the strength to overcome. Trust in your resilience and your power. Setbacks are opportunities for growth and obstacles are stepping stones to success. Embrace the discomfort, rise above the doubt, and let your determination shine through.

Believe in yourself and watch as you conquer the impossible.

March 30

Daffodils are one of the earliest blooms in spring and often represent hope and rebirth, but also clarity, honesty, and forthrightness. An alkaloid contained in the bulbs is used to slow progression of dementia. The scent was used in ancient herbalism to reduce anxiety. It was often used in love spells, and sometimes considered an aphrodisiac. Not just yellow, the flowers can range from white, to orange or pink. Recently a new genetically engineered blue daffodil was created in Wales.

Plants and bouquets can be used on altars or around the home to attract abundance and love.

March 31

The in-between places from literal doorways to the ephemeral twilight time between day and night have been noted as holding power by both religious practices and magical craft. Doorway protections, transformation rituals, and the concept of thinning veils between worlds are just a few examples.

Spell work might include the use of time such as midnight or dawn, or season, or physical places of crossing.

Begin to notice the thresholds that occur all around you, and the ones you cross.

April

April is a month of warming. The air, the soil, and the water drink in the fire in the sky. All the ingredients for life are returning in abundance. As you emerge into your most authentic self, take note of the animals and plants around you, in a process as old as time. Life begins again, and fresh hopes rise. Let ancient rhythms and curiosity combine to inspire you to enter the flow. Stretch your body, mind, and spirit and new and vibrant experiences will open.

April 1

The trickster archetype exists in myth and stories as a rule breaker. Their mischief carries the duality of wise and foolish, light and dark, friendly and villainous. They are the expanders of the mind. Personified as Loki in Norse mythology or Hermes in the Greek, they appear as animals as well, such as Anansi the Spider in Africa or Kitsune in Japan.

Embracing your inner trickster keeps you open-minded, prevents rigid thinking, and leads to surprising wisdom and creativity.

April 2

Besoms, also known as witches' brooms, were used in rituals of cleansing, protecting, and consecrating spaces and relationships. At the height of witchcraft persecution in Europe the image and idea of women flying on brooms entered the lore and has persisted through popular culture. Besoms were used as part of wedding ceremonies, known as jumping the broom. In symbolic magic they are used to cleanse negative energy from spaces. In Ancient Rome wise women used brooms to clear energy from the houses of newborn babies.

**What would you sweep away with
a magical broom?**

April 3

Persephone was the daughter of Demeter, goddess of nature. Various stories exist about who and what she was. The most well-known is her abduction by Hades, drawn into the underworld through a crack in the earth. Her story is violent, and she is subject to decisions outside her control, but despite it all she becomes both the Goddess of Spring and Queen of the Underworld, light and shadow.

What is done to you does not define you.
Never limit your own possibilities.

April 4

Honey and beeswax have been important to humans since the Stone Age as food, medicine, and magic. Ancient cultures around the world have sacred stories that feature bees. Egyptians, Minoans, Mayans are just a few. The Celts believed that bees could carry messages between the world of the living and the dead. Melissa is the Greek goddess of bees and was shown the uses of honey by the bees themselves. Properly stored honey can remain edible for thousands of years.

**Look for bees beginning
their pollination and nectar
collection. Use honey, beeswax,
or a bee charm in your magic.**

April 5

High magic involves ceremony, requisite tools and steps and hierarchy. It is most often associated with religion and the occult. It is a closed system with rules and protocols. Innate or wild magic, on the other hand, is often sourced from environment, ancestry, or personal experience and empowerment. Beliefs, practices, and tools are individualized and often solitary pursuits. Intention and focus are more individual. Many modern practices are hybrids of styles and approaches.

Take the magical path that is right for you. Listen to your heart and mind.

April 6

Your body is a constant alchemical miracle. It uses sixty naturally occurring elements as it creates and regenerates itself in every moment. It is the ultimate physical magic. Air, water, fire, and earth make and remake you. Every second, one million cells die. Over three billion cells are replaced daily. Neutrophils, a type of white blood cell, live only a few hours. Neurons are the longest living, forming in gestation and lasting a lifetime.

Treat your body as the amazing vehicle it is. Care for and respect the miracle of you.

April 7

The world is vibrant, changeable, and rushing to aliveness in the spring. Time to expand your ability to use your senses. Apply your focus and spend a few minutes each day using each sense to assess your surroundings. Hear beyond the noise to its components. Notice light and color and movement. Feel the temperature and textures. Discern scents in the air. Savor foods. Discover the layers of information all around you.

Sensory practice increases instincts and situational awareness.

April 8

Rabbits have a strong association with spring and witchcraft and are the symbol of the Germanic goddess Eostra. Folklore from Asia and indigenous America associates them with the moon and transformation. They were once believed to be familiars or even witches who had shapeshifted in order to travel safely. Symbols of abundance, fertility, and new beginnings, they are considered to be good luck. Rabbits make their homes underground and are pros at emergence, live by their wits and agility, know how to play and run. They are thrivers.

**How can you use rabbit
energy to thrive?**

April 9

Familiars have been envisaged as both guardian spirits and demons from hell. While most often they are associated with cats, they may be birds, insects, and animals both wild and domestic, and even mythical beings like dragons. Familiars are said to sometimes show up unexpectedly and adopt a person. If you could choose any familiar companion, what would it be?

Consider the creatures you have loved or cared for, and your connection. Pay attention if something adopts you, or a type of animal keeps showing up.

April 10

There are times when we must find the strength to let go and the wisdom to patiently wait for what we truly deserve. It takes courage to release what no longer serves us, and trust that something better is on its way. Letting go doesn't mean giving up; it means making space for new opportunities and blessings. Be strong enough to embrace the unknown and wise enough to wait for the perfect timing.

**Sometimes waiting patiently is
part of the process.**

April 11

With April showers comes the chance to make some Rain magic. From spells to ritual to meditation, rain can provide inspiration. Walking a labyrinth in the rain for clarity, dancing in a downpour for cleansing and release, or collecting water for ritual use are just a few ways to use this season's weather to practice, celebrate, and connect. The symbol of rain can mean abundance, fertility, renewal and coming change.

Watch it rain. Explore it with your senses. Visualize it renewing and cleansing the earth.

April 12

Casting a circle is an intentional creation of space for ritual or magical workings. The simplest casts are visualization or walking the edge of the circle. They can be spiritually cast with a pointed finger or the use of a wand. Physically they can be placed on the ground sometimes using salt, chalk, flour, water, or ash. Often the cardinal directions are indicated. The cast circle holds intention, and is intention itself.

Flower petals, stones and crystals, or fresh herbs and greenery make a pretty spring circle.

April 13

Apotropaic magic is meant to prevent or deflect harm. It is practiced in many ways such as crossing fingers, signing or inscribing symbols, charms, amulets, or rituals. Fire has been used in protective magic across cultures to prevent and cure illness in people and livestock, and smoke and ash were thought to carry that same power. Water has been similarly used in ceremonies of protection such as baptisms or initiations. Adornments and tattoos were used in some cultures as measures of protection. Warding is the use of magic for protection.

Boundaries are protection magic.

April 14

Maria Prophetissa, or Miriam the Prophetess, lived in 1st century Alexandria, Egypt, and is considered the mother of alchemy. Several alchemical inventions are credited to her and she is mentioned in the oldest books on the subject. Her writings were the first to describe distillation, and she used an alembic still to extract essences, or essential oils from flowers. Her work laid the groundwork for what was later to become the science of chemistry and some of her inventions are still used in laboratories today.

Women have made huge contributions to science across centuries.

April 15

Singing bowls likely originated in ancient Mesopotamia but the exact nature of their use has been lost. Tibetan singing bowls date to the Bon Culture and are found across Himalayan cultures. The bowls are actually a type of standing bell and the sound is produced by striking or rubbing the rim with a mallet. They are used for ceremonies, meditation, and healing.

Singing bowls can be used to reduce pain, induce relaxation, and deepen meditation.

April 16

Breathwork as part of yoga has existed for 5000 years. Spiritual teachers have long used it and even modern medicine employs it for its benefits to mental and physical health. Slow breathing exercises activate the parasympathetic nervous system lowering heart rate and blood pressure. Conversely, controlled hyperventilation stimulates the sympathetic nervous system improving focus and energy. Many types of breathwork exist and benefit in different ways.

**Explore breathwork considering
your needs to soothe or
stimulate your energy.**

April 17

Scrying is the practice of divination using a reflective or refractive surface, fire, or smoke. The seer uses an induced trance state to see and interpret visions. Objects specifically made for scrying include crystal balls or shiny spheres, scrying bowls, and black mirrors. Natural scrying uses the surface of a lake or pond, peering into fire or a candle, or observing smoke. Scrying could be used not just for predicting the future, but for seeking answers in the past or present.

The oldest historical references of scrying come from the Ancient Babylonians who used water poured on oil and interpreted the shapes they saw.

April 18

Mystics are people who have experiences of deep spiritual connection outside of structured religious practices. While mystics may follow a particular religion, they surrender to mysteries that exist beyond holy text and dogma. They feel and trust the noetic quality of deep knowing beyond the five senses. Hildegarde of Bingen, Teresa of Avila, and Joan of Arc are a few famous female mystics.

A mystical path is one of embracing the mysteries, surrendering to personal spiritual experience, and living in wonder.

April 19

Cord or Knot magic is the simple act of tying or untying knots on string, rope, hair or other strands as part of a spell or ritual. Sometimes the cords are cut to dissolve a spell or curse or modernly to excise a trauma or unwanted emotional link. Used for weather craft they can leash or set free the wind. Tied ribbons were used as love charms. Knots are used for sealing, casting, protection, and binding.

Macrame, friendship bracelets, or even shoestrings can be tied with intention.

April 20

Make friends with your body. Give yourself permission to take a break when you need it. Sometimes, we get caught up in powering through projects or missions, so listen to your body's signals and rest when necessary. Remember, self-care is a vital part of nurturing your well-being. Take time to recharge, relax, and rejuvenate. Not doing so may result in time spent dealing with illness.

**Honor your body's needs and watch
how it supports you back with
renewed energy and resilience.**

April 21

In every challenging situation, obstacles and desired outcomes coexist. Darkness brings the gift of transformation, but it's crucial to stay focused on the light, your desired outcome. Embrace the challenge as an opportunity to transform and grow. Let it shape you into a stronger version of yourself. The journey holds valuable lessons and opportunities for growth. Trust in your ability to turn obstacles into stepping stones towards success.

Carry a smooth stone as a reminder.

April 22

The 13th-century alchemist, Albertus Magnus called the use of scented smoke for magical purposes perfuming. Native Americans use smudging to purify and protect. Incense is used in religious ritual worldwide. We have long believed in the magical properties of smoke. Burning psychoactive plants to induce trances has been practiced since antiquity.

Use incense and herbs to incorporate smoke into your rituals, spells, or visualizations.

April 23

The cauldron is an important element in Welsh and Irish myth, and was variously considered to bring wisdom, endless plenty or even return from death. In magical craft it is a symbol of transformation and the divine feminine and is associated with both fire and water elements.

Large cauldrons can be filled with water and herbs for outside ceremonies or magical cooking. Small ones can be used for incense and personal spell work or on altars. A simmer pot can be used to add everyday magic to your space.

April 24

Queen Boudica was an Inceni leader famous for rebelling against Roman rule. Upon the death of her husband her lands were taken, she was beaten, and her two young daughters were raped. She raised armies to avenge them. Under her command three cities, including London were conquered and destroyed. She remains symbolic of fearless femininity in the face of patriarchal abuses.

Boudica is said to have called upon Andraste, a war goddess, and divined using a hare, sacred to the goddess.

April 25

Wands, staves and scepters have a long history in magical use with rods being found in prehistoric burials, and apotropaic wands made of hippopotamus tusk were used in birth rituals in Middle Kingdom Egypt. Homer wrote that wands were used by Hermes, Athena, and Circe. Third century depictions of Jesus show him using a wand when raising Lazurus and feeding the multitude.

Wands are used as an extension of power in casting protections, spells, and circles.

April 26

Vervain, Verbena officinalis, is known as Enchanter's Herb. A Mediterranean native, it has become naturalized in many places. It has tall white or lilac flowers. Traditionally used as nerve tonic and fever tea, studies show potential for many more benefits. It has been used historically in temples, for purification of sacred space, and carried by Roman soldiers for protection. Blacksmiths believed it strengthened the weapons they made when cooled in verbena water. Once considered a strong aphrodisiac, it was sometimes mixed into wedding flowers.

In the Middle Ages verbena was used in charms and love potions, and to enchant.

April 27

At any given moment, you are a paradox. Seemingly contradictory. It is how you are made. To be able to live and thrive even when hurting and healing. No matter how broken you may feel, you are still brave and strong at the same time. Focus on the brave and the strong and the broken will heal. You were made for these times. Be the paradox with resolve and receive the abundance that is meant for you.

**Wholeness includes your
darkness and your light.**

April 28

Flora, Roman goddess of flowers and spring, was celebrated during the festival of Floralia between April 28 and May 3. Spring is the season for discovering the power in flower craft. Create simple spells of your own intent and shaping using fresh or dried flowers. Stir petals into a bath ritual. Pair floral pastel candles with meditation. Wear floral jewelry or clothing. Go on a wildflower hunt.

**Pick up your spring magic, gently.
Let the energy of blooming guide
you. Let yourself open.**

April 29

About forty percent of all birds migrate, from hummingbirds weighing ounces to geese weighing pounds. Migration routes can take them as far as 16,000 miles. Some fly several hundred feet above the ground while others are up as high as airliners.

In myth and magic birds can symbolize renewal or transition of the soul, bring messages, or as familiars.

What bird resonates with your magic? Learn about the species or create a sigil.

April 30

You are on a journey, a path that is entirely yours. It's essential to recognize the significance of this journey and to understand your reasons for doing the work you do. There may be times when you feel like giving up or quitting, but remember that sometimes, your miracle is just one step away. Take a moment to reflect on why you started. Reignite that fire within you and let it guide you towards your goals.

Stop to rest when you need to, and you will find the strength to continue. Drive yourself to exhaustion and you will quit, erroneously believing you were defeated.

May

Beltane, the ancient fire festival, is an invitation to step into your magical awareness and power. Life pushes forward at a faster pace. Birds are singing, flowers are opening, and the leaves on the trees find their deep green. The energy that comes at the end of spring makes it a perfect time to explore your song, and your blossoming. Find your deepest colors. Become lush. Begin to inquire into the many ways to touch and grow your magic.

May 1

Beltane opens the month of May, considered the first of summer in Ireland and Scotland. Halfway between spring equinox and summer solstice, it is a festival of fire, fertility, abundance, and the growing power of the sun. Consider what you want from the summer season, your goals and your challenges. Write in a vision book or journal. When you are clear on your intentions, design a ritual, work a spell or choose a symbol to aid manifestation.

Practice your magic.

May 2

The Hawthorn tree is historically a magical tree, and its blossoming was a traditional sign of Beltane when the flowers would be gathered. They are also said to be protected by fairies and were used as border hedges. Hawthorn in magical use existed in many places around the world, often associated with self-love, acceptance, and courage. During the Middle Ages it was used in Christian protective magic and hung over doorways. Today it is recognized for its nutritive and medicinal properties.

Hawthorn flowers, berries or thorns are used in modern spells, rituals, and altar decoration.

May 3

Combining herbs with water creates infusions and decoctions. Teas, or infusions, are steeped in water, either boiling or cold depending on the plant properties. Decoctions are brought to a boil and simmered and generally used for tougher plant parts such as roots, berries, bark, seeds, and mushrooms. This is a basic extraction method for various herbal medicine practices.

Learn more about herbal preparations, or incorporate tea into a spell, practice, or ritual.

May 4

Singing, humming, or chanting can be incorporated into almost every magical craft and are often used in many religious and healing settings. They also have effects on the brain and body, particularly the vagus nerve, reducing stress hormones and increasing pleasure hormones. Songs can be added to spells or be the spell themselves.

**Find and exercise your voice,
whether that involves a voice coach
or singing alone in the car. If you
don't want to sing, just hum.**

May 5

Life is too short to spend it doing things that don't bring you joy. Follow your passions, pursue your dreams, and embrace the things that make your heart sing. Whether it's painting, writing, singing, or simply spending time with loved ones, make time for the activities that truly light you up. The time you spend doing what you love is never wasted. It fills your soul, sparks creativity, and brings a sense of purpose to your days.

**Living with passion invites joy
into your life.**

May 6

Legend says that Aurora, goddess of the Dawn, rises from the sea each morning riding her chariot into the sky. She carries a pitcher from which she sprinkles the earth with dew. Dew is used in magical practices, with that gathered in the spring considered most potent. Dabbed on the third eye it is said to increase psychic ability. Washing one's face in dew is used for glamour.

Collect dew in a bottle or on cloth and use it magically.

May 7

Your voice is a force that can create ripples of change in the world. Speak up against injustice, share your experiences, and stand tall for what you believe in. You have the ability to inspire, empower, and uplift. Whether it's through art, writing, or even a simple conversation, let your voice be heard. Use it as a tool to break barriers, challenge norms, and push boundaries.

**Embrace your uniqueness
and let the world witness your
authenticity.**

May 8

When the soil warms, gardeners and farmers begin their work. The soil is turned, weeds and debris are cleared, seeds are planted. They are little things that don't look anything like what they will become in the summer ahead. Small actions create the same explosion of growth. Embrace this time of planting for future harvest. Focus your intent.

If your life were a garden, what seeds would you plant, how would you prepare the soil? Choose what nourishes your whole self and begin.

May 9

The Phoenix is a sacred Firebird that rises from the ashes of death after burning the old self away. It symbolizes immortality, rebirth, and renewal. At each stage of our lives we must recreate ourselves anew, letting go of old ways to grow healthily. The very cells that make our bodies are dying and renewing all the time. Our mental and spiritual regeneration is just as important.

Write a poem about the changes you've experienced. Candle gaze while meditating on the next stage.

May 10

There is power in setting your unbending intent. When you have a specific desire in mind, let your intention be unwavering. Trust in the universe's guidance and surrender to its wisdom. Take consistent action towards your goal, while remaining open to the unexpected blessings and opportunities that come your way.

**Trust that the universe is
conspiring in your favor, align
your actions with your intentions,
and let the magic happen!**

May 11

Our energy naturally increases with the lengthening days, and we tend to become more active. It is a good time to explore our sourcing and see the times and places in our lives where energy comes without pushing it. What restores your vigor and lifeforce? Do you find it easy or difficult to increase your power supply when needed? If more energy is needed it may require better nutrition, movement or meditation. Or it may signal a need to rediscover joy.

**What makes your soul sing?
What people, places, or pursuits
feel restorative?**

May 12

Success in life, love or magic all depend on showing up and doing the work. After the need for survival, passion and purpose are powerful motivations for consistency. We must invest time, energy, and action in the areas we want to thrive. What passions and purpose are you following? Are they conscious or are you being passive with your life? Are you investing in yourself?

**Commit to working toward that
which you feel deeply about.
Small steps count.**

May 13

Maia was a goddess of springtime who lends her name to the month of May. She later became known as Bona Dea, meaning the good goddess, whose name was too sacred to speak aloud. She embodied earth and growth and gently growing heat, and her observances were female dominated. Maia is variously described as nurturer, mother, and midwife, and associated with knotted and braided items such as hair and ribbons.

In honor of the nurturing women in your life, have a dinner celebrating them, or give gifts of flowers tied with ribbons and good intentions. Braid intention into hair.

May 14

The word Dryad originally meant a nymph of an oak tree but has become a term used for all tree spirits. They are thought to protect the forests and woodlands and are in communication with all the creatures who live there. Science has found that trees send signals to one another through chemicals. In addition to all the senses we have, trees can also detect gravity and light we cannot.

Take a walk among the trees and consider that they may be more aware of you than they seem.

May 15

Runes are letters of an alphabet of angular script used to write early Germanic languages and stemming from the Phoenician. The meaning of the word itself suggests secrecy and mystery and it is possible they were intended more for magical charms than everyday writing. Their use in divination was written about by Tacitus in 98CE. In Viking beliefs, runes were given to the world by Odin the Allfather.

In addition to divination runes are worn for protection or luck and as magical inscriptions on objects and markers.

May 16

Failure is never the end of the road. Success is not always immediate or permanent, but what matters is having the courage to keep going. Those moments of setbacks and challenges are how we learn, grow, and evolve. Embrace the lessons, gather the strength, and keep moving forward. It's not about falling but rising, with new knowledge and renewed resolve.

Be bold, be resilient, and show the world what you're made of.

May 17

Alchemilla is the Latin name for Lady's Mantle and means little alchemist or little magical one. It is a herbaceous perennial in the rose family. Its velvety leaves are covered in tiny hairs that capture and hold water. Alchemists believed dew from the plant was powerful magic. Women collected the dew for beauty spells. It was used by midwives for childbirth and women's health. It is also associated with love and fertility spells, and is a symbol of femininity.

**In modern practices it is used
as an enhancing ingredient.
Planted in the garden it protects
against negative magic.**

May 18

When water collides with itself such as waterfalls, waves, and rain, negative ions are released, sometimes called the Waterfall Effect. Ions are electrically charged atoms that are invisible, odorless, and tasteless. Breathing them in creates a feeling of wellness, increases energy and enhances alertness. Research shows benefits for sleep patterns, mood, and immune function. Hot water and steam in the shower offers healthy benefits too. Negative ions can be found in abundance in dense forests and mountains as well.

Get into nature and breathe in wellness and energy.

May 19

Being a realist doesn't mean dwelling on the negatives. It's about seeing things as they are, acknowledging both the challenges and the opportunities. By embracing realism, you gain the power to navigate life with clarity and adaptability, make informed decisions, set realistic goals, and take steps towards your dreams. Avoid lying to yourself to remain in a comfort zone. You will not be safer or happier.

Embracing the totality of the present moment crafts a future guided by your aspirations instead of your fears.

May 20

Jade has been carved for sacred and ritual use for more than five thousand years in China. The Aztecs used jade in rituals for gods and royalty. It was considered more valuable than gold by the Mayans. It comes in several colors ranging from green to violet to white and is very hard. Stone Age peoples used it to make tools and weapons. Neo-pagans use jade for dreamwork and connecting to ancestral knowledge.

Wear jade for good luck as charms and amulets. Gift it for friendship.

May 21

Social gatherings increase with the warmer seasons. This is a chance to practice your skills of observation both in the natural world and in interactions with people. Use each of your senses and your instincts to feel the energy around you and note when it changes. People watch during celebrations, and ceremonies. Look for signs of emotions and attitudes and become aware when yours change in response. Remain an observer. Learn what people's buttons are, and what yours are as well.

**Practice at reading people involves
body, mind, and spirit at once.
Observation aids intuition.**

May 22

Near the end of every season is a good time to consider your energy levels. Look at where you expend your energy, how and when you receive it, and where in your life you need more. Where are you changing and where are you stuck? Check in with your health and your mindset. Spend some quiet time with yourself, without agenda, and see what comes up.

What would it look like to focus your magic on a healthier, happier you?

May 23

Have you ever considered your particular natural magic? That skill or talent that comes so effortlessly to you, but leaves others in awe? It could be as simple as the ability to make people laugh or your ability for creative problem-solving. Everyone has gifts. We each have to open them ourselves.

Consider how you can benefit yourself or others by developing what is naturally yours.

Dismissing the value of your talents is self-sabotage, and keeps you from sharing the best of you with the world.

May 24

Do you often hesitate to ask for what you truly want? Are you unsure if you can actually attain it or if you even deserve it? This a gentle reminder to dare to ask for what you desire, and nothing less. You are worthy of all the goodness and happiness that life has to offer. So go ahead, embrace your worthiness and let the world see it, too. Will you help yourself, or wait to see if your wishes come to you?

I am worthy, capable, and powerful.

May 25

Tokens, charms and talismans worn on the body call attention both subtly and overtly, causing you to think differently and more often about your magic, and its place in your life. Symbolism and repetition can change the brain and create a constant energy we can use for our empowerment. What needs repeating? What message do you know you need to keep in the forefront of your mind? What symbolizes your strength, your talent, or your passion?

**Send messages to yourself
using symbols and tokens
worn or kept close.**

May 26

Every day, every moment holds a special kind of magic that is uniquely yours. Each second is an opportunity to create something amazing, to chase your dreams, and to experience joy and fulfillment. So seize the magic by making the most of every day, and watch your life transform into something truly extraordinary. This life is yours. No one else is you.

You have the power within you to create your own unique magic.

May 27

Jar spells are simply bottled spells. They can contain almost anything that resonates with your intentions including natural items, writing, tokens, and personal objects like jewelry. They are limited only by your creativity. Once complete they can be a reminder of your purpose, or in the case of banishing, binding or protective warding they can be buried or otherwise removed from sight. Seasonal themed jars can be a way to remember to stay present and attuned to the everchanging year.

Consider which small items and ingredients you would include in a personal seasonal jar for spring.

May 28

Sunrise is a perfect time to explore the magic of beginnings. Early morning solitude often provides clarity and is a good time to journal or write correspondence. Sun salutations, yoga, or a tea ceremony can set the tone for a calmly productive day. A run can invigorate the body. How you interact with and use morning magic is up to you. Embrace and accept the possibilities each new day brings.

**Set your intentions and make
fresh magic daily.**

May 29

The power of discernment, to grasp what is real and possible on a deeper level than we tend to with numbed or conditioned thinking, is a power that can be practiced and increased. Not everything in life is straightforward or clear, and it is the ability to discern that helps us untangle those difficulties. Know that you have prejudices and preferences that affect your rational decision making. Question your own motives and methods. Look for signs of falsity and danger in the world, but also opportunity. Look beyond the obvious.

Zoom out. See the bigger picture. Zoom in and look at the fine details.

May 30

Life doesn't just happen to us; we have the power to become active participants in how we interpret and deal with the circumstances that come our way. By shifting our mindset and taking ownership of our responses, we can find strength, resilience, and ultimately, the ability to shape our own destiny. Embracing this empowering perspective enables us to use the only control we have, which is in the here and now. We cannot change the past, but we can affect our future with choices we make today.

Your life is right now, and that is also where your power is.

May 31

This season moved you from out of the deep dreaming and darkness of winter through the incremental transition to warmth and light. Now spring has brought you to the edge of summer, with unknown wild growth and endless possibilities before you. Ease into the transition but begin to shift. Take your spring lessons and skills forward into the creative energy of the summer sun.

Light a candle or create a ceremony acknowledging both what you have gained from and what you released this season.

The Summer Witch

The Summer Witch is both sunshine and storm, pulled by both fire and water, golden days and velvet nights. There is sureness in the Summer Witch and she is aware of both her inner and her outer world. Summer holds abundance and lushness for the senses and the Summer Witch draws this power, steps into the sensual and embraces her Audacious Authenticity. These are the days to live under the sun and the stars, to grow bolder and braver. The Summer Witch discovers her strengths and embraces them. She is the boldest of her season sisters, capable of deep love, and fierce protection.

Embrace and Celebrate
Summer Magic

- Go on a picnic.
- Stargaze.
- Start a garden.
- Visit farmer's markets.
- Watch a thunderstorm.
- Immerse in a lake, a pool, or the ocean
- Make a summer reading list
- Visit a public garden.
- Create a playlist of songs about fire.

Symbols, Scents, & Such

Sunshine

Fire, Dragons, a Phoenix

Mermaids, Seashells, and the Ocean

Gold, Copper

Lions

Rubies, Aquamarine

June

June ushers in summer bringing sunshine and storms, setting into motion rapid growth. It begins the most fertile and abundant season of the year. Change is everywhere as life renews itself all around. We celebrate beginnings and endings, love and accomplishments. The long days invite play. Take a break from the rigid and the mundane. Move. Explore. Adventure. Let the sun make you brave. Let the storms make you strong.

June 1

Juno was the Roman goddess of women and marriage, and many marriages still take place during this month. She was also associated with childbirth as Juna Lucina, "Juno who brings the light". On this first day of meteorological summer take time to consider what brings light into your life. Decide what you want from this season and what steps you need to take to make that happen.

Create your summer vision.
Perform a ritual or craft a spell
of intention that is all your own.
Welcome the season.

June 2

Directional movement beliefs are a part of many religious, folk, and magical practices. In a circle or around a sacred object, the deosil, or clockwise, direction is for increasing energy for positive outcomes such as luck, protection, and healing. Widdershins, or counterclockwise, reverses, decreases, banishes, disconnects, and releases negatives. Using these associations reinforces intention and focus.

**Consider directional movement
when creating your own magic.
Move with intention.**

June 3

Roses symbolize love, passion, attraction, and sensuality, and have endless uses in magical practices. Flowers and petals can be used fresh or dried, or processed into tinctures, incense, rose water, teas or spells. Rose hips are a good source of vitamin C. Petals can be added to ritual baths. Thorns can be used in protection rituals or charm bags. Rose colors vary offering many magical correspondences for personal meanings. Romans believed roses could hold secrets wrapped in their petals.

Sub rosa means "under the rose" and denotes secret keeping and confidential matters.

June 4

Being a warrior, not a worrier, means facing life's challenges with strength and courage instead of anxiety and fear. Approaching life in this way, you can overcome obstacles and achieve goals. Being a warrior means standing up for what you believe in, setting boundaries, and advocating for your needs and those of your loved ones. Being a warrior does not mean approaching the world through anger. Anger clouds judgment.

Feed your courage. Starve your fear.

June 5

June is full of beginnings and endings, and those thresholds are often important life moments like weddings and graduations. Amidst the celebrations there are often nerves or uncertainties about what comes next. Instead of anxiety about the past or present, practice the art of being in the moment. It is good to remember, and it is good to plan, but never lose sight of the power of now. Life is a constant state of change. Being present allows for thoughtful adaptation.

This moment is the only moment in which you have any control.

June 6

Summer camp is all about fresh air, nature, learning new things, and growing healthy and strong, and hopefully making friends. While you may not be able to take a month to go on retreat, consider ways to recreate the experience. What activities would you have in your ideal summer camp? What new skill would you learn? What favorite activity from your youth would you like to enjoy again? Give yourself the gift of simple pursuits and pleasures. Slow down.

**Summer days and nights are perfect
for making happy memories.**

June 7

In Norse mythology, the Norns are three sisters who together determine human fate. Urd, Skuld, and Verdandi are beings of time and destiny. They tend to the roots of Yggdrasil, the tree of Life. They weave the tapestry of life, giving each individual a thread. One sister spins, one measures, and one cuts each destiny. The Old Norse word norn means both weaver and worker of magic.

Some things you will be able to control, others you won't. Your destiny is decided by the choices you make in both cases.

June 8

Despite fragile looking blooms the Lotus flower has been around for millions of years and survived the ice age. Today it can be found in places as disparate as East Africa, Russia, Australia and the Middle East. A Sacred Lotus rises from the mud to bloom, closes to sink beneath the water each night, only to rise clean again. White or Egyptian Lotus bloom at night and close in the day. Symbols of rebirth and purity, their seeds stay viable for centuries.

Do you bloom in the day or the night?

June 9

Mead is fermented from honey and may be the world's oldest alcoholic drink, so old that the exact origins are unknown. It was consumed by ancient Egyptians and Greeks as well as the Mayans. In Medieval Europe mead was given to newlyweds to drink for fertility and happiness and may be where the term honeymoon originates. Favored by Vikings for feasting and ritual, it was believed by Celts to deliver magical powers. Today many varieties of mead can be found.

Mead is a traditional drink to celebrate summer solstice.

June 10

Thunderstorms were once thought to be due to the activities of the gods. Science teaches about their natural power, and while potentially destructive, they are necessary to maintain the electrical balance between the earth and its atmosphere. Culturally, they have been interpreted as symbols of both destruction and transformation. Intense and powerful, thunderstorms are change makers. Some people fear them, others are enchanted. How they make you feel determines how you will use them in your magic.

**How do you interpret the energy
and atmosphere of storms?**

June 11

Our attitude is where our energy meets the world. It is affected by emotions, beliefs, and biology. When we are open and flexible we are able to evaluate and take advantage of opportunities. When we are closed and rigid, we shut the door on our options. Our attitude determines the quality of our relationships, our work, our health and our lives. Our mental approach can be an asset or a detriment. Adjusting our attitude can remove blockages and promote flow.

Get out of your own way.

June 12

Skin cells have olfactory sensors for the scent of sandalwood. Unlike scent receptors in the nose these messages aren't sent to the brain but directly to the cells, triggering cell proliferation and healing. Used ritually and medicinally for thousands of years, it induces a calm and meditative state. It was also used in anointing and burial practices. Indian sandalwood is endangered and the most commercially available product comes from Australia.

**Warm and woody, sandalwood
is alluring. Try it as a perfume,
candle, incense, or body oil.**

June 13

You are designed with a unique purpose for a unique experience. Your heart is the guidance system providing you with desires that are guideposts to living your purposeful life. Your mind is the mechanism that allows you to discover who you are meant to be. The longings and callings are trying to pull you in the direction of your purpose. Your focus should be on your path, not anyone else's. It is not a competition. You don't require validation or permission to be fully yourself.

Your purpose won't look exactly like anyone else's.

June 14

The life of the butterfly is one of constant change. From egg to caterpillar to chrysalis to winged butterfly, it experiences multiple transformations, completely undoing its own structure and becoming essential goo. Through a radical set of changes it becomes more of itself with each rebirth, and ultimately gains wings. What have been the stages of your metamorphosis? Can you recall the transitions that have gotten you here? Are you ready to fly?

Russian folklore suggests that butterflies are witches in disguise. Aztec beliefs held that butterflies escorted souls of those lost in battle or childbirth to their rest.

June 15

Freya is the Norse goddess of magic, witchcraft, love, warfare, sex, fertility, death, and beauty. Beloved from Scandinavia to Iceland to Holland and Britain she was named Queen of the Witches by Christian authorities who feared her influence and autonomy. Daughter of the Sea and the Earth she was of the Vanir, a group of Norse gods, and was born knowing runecraft and magic and with the ability to change fate.

**Her sacred flowers are daisy
and primrose.**

June 16

The sun has been seen as divine power for millennia. Ancient solar symbols date from Mesopotamia but are found in many ancient cultures. Sun energy in magic is associated with growth, health and abundance but also cleansing. What areas of your life would benefit from some sunshine? What shadows could be swept aside? Experiment with ways to use this energy in your life. Meditate on sunbeams. Plant sunflowers. Design your own sun sigil or make sun tea. Feel its warmth on your skin.

Power word: Shine.

June 17

It is hard to maintain our energy level sometimes, and often we can't lessen our responsibilities despite feeling drained. That is why we need to look for places and ways our precious resources get wasted. We all need rest and sustenance for energy, but less obvious are our energy costs and outlays. Where are you costing yourself? Where do you need to make adjustments?

Complaining, overthinking, inability to release what doesn't serve, and unhealthy relationships decrease your power.

June 18

Magical springs send water bubbling out of the earth from deep down in the aquifers. Fresh water springs and wells have always been considered sacred and were some of the earliest ritual sites. Stories of miracles, healing and visions surround these places. Offerings of weapons of valuables would be made for divine intervention or as gifts for water spirits.

Spring water's magical uses include healing, love and glamour potions, cleansing, luck, and divination.

June 19

Sometimes life is chaotic and unpredictable, but it is important to appreciate the beauty in the chaos. In the midst of uncertainty, we learn to adapt, grow, and become stronger. When things don't go as planned, it can actually be a gift in disguise. It's through challenges and unexpected twists and turns that we build strength and resilience.

Embrace the chaos and trust in the journey, because it's all leading you exactly where you're meant to be.

June 20

If you look up the definition for self-centered you will see several negative phrases, most indicating a lack of care for others. The truth is that self-centering is self-sufficiency and independence of thought that can strengthen relationships, balance emotions, and increase wellbeing. It requires introspection and honesty about your beliefs and priorities, then aligning your actions with your center.

**When we act and think from our core,
we best serve ourselves and others.**

June 21

Summer solstice is the longest day, when the sun is at full strength and associated with ancient temple and monument alignments around the globe. It is a good day to set intentions and goals for the season or make a list of things you would like to experience this summer. If this is the high season for energy, how will you use it?

**Light a candle or bonfire.
Meditate on your inner fire and
power and how you will use it for
your highest good.**

June 22

The element of water is powerful in its ability to flow around difficulty, to shape shift according to its need. It is flexible and adaptable. Magically it is used for cleansing, divination, and ritual. The type of water can determine function. Clear water is purifying or clarifying. Dirty water is occluding. Salt, spring, lake, or river waters carry distinct energies.

Incorporate water energy with magical practice when bathing or drinking. Make flower or moon water.

June 23

On Midsummer's eve ancient people would light bonfires and dance through the night. Even today this bonfire holiday takes place in many countries around the world. Traditional rituals include greeting the dawn for health, gathering flowers for spells and love potions, and dream work. Midsummer has long been considered to be one of the times of year when magic is most potent.

**Host or attend a bonfire, or
light a candle, open the window
and read Shakespeare's A
Midsummer Night's Dream.**

June 24

Aine was a powerful Celtic goddess of Summer and wealth. She represents the sun, love, abundant crops and good harvests. Like many females in myth and history she was a victim of violence. Her revenge brought down a King and her legend tells of her ability to grant personal power and sovereignty. She is also known as Queen of the Fairies, and Aine of the Light, and was likely worshiped as far back as the Neolithic Age.

What abundance do you call into your life this season of growth? Will you grant yourself access to your power and claim your own crown?

June 25

It's time to break free from the chains of needing permission to be your truest self. No more wasting precious moments seeking validation from others. Instead embark on a journey of self-discovery. Your uniqueness is a gift. Seek to know yourself. Dive into the depths of your being to see your true desires, strengths, and values. Know that you have the power within you to create your own path and a life that aligns with your true essence.

Pay special attention to whatever moves your heart to joy.

June 26

Dragonflies have been a part of our world before species of flying animals in prehistoric times. Their physical presence brings a mystical and mysterious view of a creature who can see 360 degrees at once. They are an invitation to us to be aware of the limited focus we may have of our lives and our world. Because of their short lifespans, they also remind us that we need to open our minds and hearts to the fact that we all have an expiration date.

Be a dragonfly or damselfly today and open to the whole of your existence and the need to be present now.

June 27

With the abundance of fresh food available in summer it is a great time to embrace the practice of seasonal eating. Not only is fresh food more nutritious but eating food in season is an easy way to engage with and celebrate the rhythms of the year. For ancient peoples both staple and celebratory foods relied on availability, and many rituals reflect those traditions even today in feasts and offerings. What is your favorite summer food?

Visit a pick-your-own berry farm or a farmer's market. Develop your own recipes or plan a seasonal food dinner party.

June 28

Deadly Nightshade, also known as Belladonna meaning beautiful woman, is a highly poisonous plant in the Solanaceae family. All parts of the plant are toxic. Despite this, it has a history of both cosmetic and medicinal use, having been used as a hallucinogen since antiquity. Delirium can last for days. It was once believed to be a key ingredient in witch's flying ointment.

Other members of the nightshade family include tomatoes, eggplant, peppers, potatoes, and tobacco.

June 29

Procrastination is a thief, robbing you of precious time, opportunities, and potential growth. It's time to make things happen. No more waiting. Having a plan isn't about creating something pretty on paper. It's about taking that plan, breathing life into it, and turning it into reality. Action is the key to success and magic. Rise above the lure of procrastination.

Whether it's an idea you've been nurturing or a goal you've been putting off, the time to act is now.

June 30

It is crucial to recognize the immense influence you have over your own experiences. By taking complete responsibility for your choices, you unleash the potential for growth and transformation. You hold the key to manifesting the life you desire. So, dare to be responsible for who you are and how you navigate through this world.

Embracing risks, challenges, and triumphs will unfold extraordinary miracles.

July

July is a golden month when the sun is a mighty lion, at the height of its power. There is a sense of freedom in deep summer that invites you to live magically, and joyfully co-create with the universe. It is a month of light - dazzling sunsets and sunrises, silent fireflies, and exploding firecrackers. It is a time when all things seem possible, when we dare to embody the spirit, we are. July offers adventure and risk, a high dive into who we are meant to be.

July 1

It is believed the first firecrackers were used in ancient China and were simply lengths of bamboo that would explode when thrown in the fire, thereby expelling evil spirits. Then an alchemist compounded gunpowder and added it to the bamboo sticks. Later they were wrapped in paper, and created what we call fireworks. Boom! What negativity would you like to expel in your life?

If you could throw magical firecrackers and dispel negativity in your life, where would you aim?

July 2

Amaterasu is a goddess of the sun who appears in the earliest Japanese literary writings. Her name means "to illuminate" or "shines in the sky," and she is sister to the moon god and the storm god. Her symbols are a mirror, a sword and a necklace. The Ise Grand Shrine in Japan must have a priest or priestess from the Imperial family, and Amaterasu is still part of the spiritual culture today.

What in your life could benefit from illumination. What needs to be brought into the light of day?

July 3

Gold has been prized since antiquity for magic, medicine, and as a sign of status. From decoration to coronation to burials, the use of gold in ritual is found all over the world. Its use in magic items varies just as widely. Amulets, talismans, vessels, and spells made use of the powers of gold to call in abundance, love, or protection. It is one of the seven metals of alchemy. It symbolizes the sun, power, and wealth. Gold is only created by supernova explosions or collisions of neutron stars. Earth's gold is made of long dead stars.

How will you use gold in your magical work?

July 4

Fully embracing your own power to affect your life and claiming your agency and independence will take you to a higher level of understanding and accomplishment. No one can increase your skills for you. No one else can learn or be responsible for what you need to know. It means moving beyond fear, and no longer making yourself small. It means choosing and acting in ways that support your success.

Ask yourself what you need to know or do to have the life you want to have.

July 5

The ocean is the perfect place to practice summer magic. The energy of the waves, the salt water, and the vastness of the sea and its creatures invigorate the body and the imagination. Beneath the sea lies a world of beauty and mystery. Just like inside you.

Simply writing in the sand and letting the waves take the words is magic. Casting stones into the waves can be an act of release or healing. Breathing the air and bathing in the water is restorative. Embrace your inner Sea Witch.

July 6

Life has a way of surprising us. Sometimes, it feels like the very fabric of our existence is being torn apart by circumstances beyond our control. We find ourselves standing in the middle of a gap between our "old" and "new" lives, unsure of what lies ahead. This space holds the opportunity to write the next chapter of your story. Don't be afraid to pick up the pen.

Every conscious choice you make is a stepping stone towards a brighter future. Breathe and summon the courage within.

July 7

Seashells are a perfect small item to use for seasonal altars, life boards, spells, amulets, or charms. They can be worn, carried, or displayed where they catch your eye in manifestation magic. Simply cast into the ocean they can carry a wish or a spell. Both Aphrodite and Venus are associated with shells. Shells have been used around the world as currency, tools, and even musical instruments for ritual use.

An eighteen-thousand-year-old conch shell with holes drilled precisely to produce musical notes was found far from the ocean during the excavation of a cave in the French Pyrenees.

July 8

Granny Magic, also known as Granny Witchcraft, is a type of folk magic practiced in the Appalachian Mountains. Older women in the communities, called Grannies, served as midwives and healers. A blend of Native American, European, and African knowledge, their cures and treatments included herbal methods of contraception and abortion. Between 1860 and 1890 there was a movement to eliminate midwives and put women's reproductive care and control in the hands of doctors.

By the turn of the century men presided at half of US births, despite little obstetrics training.

July 9

Pearls are the only gemstone formed by a living creature, born of the sea and not in the soil. Symbolic of transformation and accumulated wisdom they are luminescent and beautiful. Before they can be used for adornment or riches they must be brought from the deep. Like many treasures they must be worked for. You will not find them on the shore. Be prepared to go diving.

Margaritomancy is the use of pearls for divination.

July 10

Henbane was one of the most important drugs in ancient times for pain relief as well as calming the mind. Black, yellow and white flower varieties were used as both medicine and poison. Highly toxic, it could also be used to induce trances and hallucinations and earned the name of Witch's Herb. The sensation of flying helped lead to the broomstick riding witch archetype.

Druids and Vikings buried the seeds of henbane with their dead.

July 11

Summer energy supports taking risks and having experiences. It's the time to do things that excite and scare you, like a child on a diving board for the first time. When we summon our courage and trust ourselves to do what is truly calling us, we still must take that leap. But when we do, even if we come up sputtering, we feel triumphant.

What have you been waiting to dive into?

Never be afraid to answer the call from yourself. That's how regrets are created.

July 12

How comfortable are you in your own naked skin? We all have attachments to issues of morals or beauty standards and have been conditioned out of self-appreciation. Your body is housing you for this experience. Are you a good tenant? Using oils, creams, and serums on the skin can be a simple but transformative ritual in body love. Learn about natural body oils and creams. Choose what is right for you. In a magic ritual, application might be combined with elements of fire or water. Try bathing with candles and adding natural healing tools or practices. Let yourself glow.

You were born naked and beautiful.

July 13

Lion images appear at the beginnings of civilization as symbols of strength and authority, ferocity, and courage. Lionesses symbolize sisterhood, feminine power, and prowess, and no less courage. They do not simply survive, they thrive, bring their pride along with them, and never lose their confidence in their own abilities to affect their existence. When faced with challenge or threat draw on your deep wild energy and leonine power.

**Wear a piece of jewelry to
remind yourself of your
strengths. Inspire yourself.**

July 14

Mermaids occur in folklore and art around the world. Sometimes they are benign but often not, mermaids are not people pleasers. In modern times they are symbols of feminine autonomy. In myths some had magical powers and could foretell the future. Often associated with music and songs, their voices were beguiling enough to lure people to their doom. They are creatures of danger, beauty, and freedom.

Where would you swim if you were a mermaid? Create your own meditation.

July 15

Courage doesn't always come easy, but every lioness must learn to roar. Our roar can be a warning, or a call to our tribe. If we feel the need to voice it, we usually have a need to protect ourselves or our loved ones. It is a different sound than the roar of the lion male's triumphant aggression. It is feminine strength and courage, tooth and claw protection. It is the roar of survival for kin and kind. It is not for show or vanity.

Trust your instincts. Trust your voice. Roar if you need to.

July 16

Life is a tapestry woven with intricate details. Paying attention to those tiny threads leads to breathtaking results. Approach every task, every interaction, and every moment with integrity and authenticity, and something magical happens. Life becomes enriched, and our experiences take on a new level of meaning and satisfaction. Let each gesture, word and decision be infused with intent.

Don't underestimate the power of details, thoughtfulness and precision.

July 17

Summer reading! Find a book that moves you. Choose a story that makes you feel and shows you something new. Reading fiction correlates with higher emotional intelligence and increase in empathy, understanding and the ability for deep and profound thinking. What book do you still love from childhood or adolescence?

Visit a library or bookstore. Take yourself on reading dates.

July 18

Children know important things. They can reteach you to be curious, to play, and to redevelop trust in your instincts. Wonder and awe stop children in their tracks so they can take it in. They aren't ashamed of what they don't know. They don't feel the need to hide their true selves or their affections. They love stories of the past, and dreams for the future. They value the simple but most important things, and they express joy easily.

Let your inner child out to play.

July 19

Sea glass was once sharp and broken. Time, water, and sand wear the cutting edges smooth. They polish the surface until it has a soft sheen. It transforms into luminous treasure. Many experiences and events can leave us with jagged and broken pieces. With care for ourselves, with connections, and with purposefully seeking beauty within and without, we can polish the edges and create new beauty for our life.

I am always becoming.

July 20

Summer is sensuous, a party for your perceptual abilities that invites you to practice your awareness. Whether seeing old things in new ways, or having new adventures altogether, gather sensory information. How does it all feel? Pay attention to how new awareness resonates, and whether your tastes change.

See how many classic summer sights, sounds, scents, tastes, and feels you can collect. Write them down.

July 21

Rubies are attributed to a large number of cultures to procure help in causes ranging from love to war. Passion, power, courage, protection, health and luck are said to be enhanced by the wearing of rubies. Both natural and synthetic rubies are used in laser technology for their ability to concentrate and intensify light. They are the traditional birthstone for July and are second in hardness only to diamonds.

Use ruby in your manifesting to concentrate and intensify your focus and energy.

July 22

Asteria was a Titan, a pre-Olympian goddess of Ancient Greece whose name means of the stars or starry one. She rules over nighttime divination and dream prophecy, astrology, and falling stars. Herbs associated with her include mugwort and wormwood. Her only daughter, Hekate, became goddess of witchcraft.

Take advantage of summer nights to lie under the stars and consider your future. Use a classic form of divination, or just stardream. Add your own magical touches such as candles or incense.

July 23

When everything spins too fast and you are caught in a whirlwind that can't be controlled, your only power lies in your response. If you can hold off panic and look around, you will find things you can use to help you. Opportunities, connections, or fresh understandings might be all around you. Don't let the power of your life scare you. Pull what you need. Repel what you don't.

Embrace the whirlwind.

July 24

Cultural myths of dragons exist in Asia, Africa, the Americas, and Europe. The oldest dragon carvings date from 4000 to 3000 BCE and are found in Mongolia. Serpentine dragons, poisonous or fire breathing exist in early myths of several civilizations, often guarding treasure. Dragon energy is highly charismatic, confident, and intelligent.

What do dragons symbolize to you? What attributes do you consider them having? Would you fight them or fly them?

July 25

The Phoenix is a sacred bird in ancient legend that lived for 500 years, growing very wise. Then when its body was old it would build a nest that would become a funeral pyre as the flames consumed it. From the ashes it would arise and a new 500-year cycle would begin. Associated with red and orange, rebirth and transformation. Like the Phoenix, human lives go through cycles of complete transformation. Our daily existence and presence changes and changes again as we grow and age.

Mantra: I will rise and begin.

July 26

Sandcastles are created knowing they are temporary and will wash away again into the sea, and still, we build them. The simple joy is in their creation. They teach us that not everything will stay in life and sometimes beautiful things end, but we can be grateful in the moment. Remaining present to the temporary beauty and goodness that we create in our lives means we don't miss a thing. Those moments and memories are ours forever if we pay attention.

As long as we live our lives are changing. Savor what is beautiful and joyful while it lasts.

July 27

Foxglove was once thought to attract fairies, and like fairies is both dangerous and useful. It is a tall plant with bell shaped flowers in a range of colors. All parts of the plant are poisonous, but it is also the source of digitalis used to treat the heart and alter its electrical activity. It has been a symbol for hedge witches, white witches, and midwives as well as a warding herb sprinkled around cradles to protect infants. Norwegian folklore tells of fairies teaching foxes to ring the flower bells to warn of danger.

Foxglove symbolizes secrets, riddles, and puzzles.

July 28

Fireflies can be found on every continent except Antarctica. emerging into the dusky evening to show their light. The Smokey Mountains and Southeast Asia each have a species that flash all together in a phenomenon of simultaneous bio-luminescence. The compound that allows for the glow is luciferin which comes from the Latin Lucifer and means 'light bearing'. Symbolism ranges across cultures from spirits of the dead to moon magic.

Create a meditation visualizing being in a forest of fireflies. What messages or gifts do their lights bring?

July 29

The ever-changing moon phases have always been connected to ritual and sacred practice. When full the moon is whole and complete then wanes to a crescent sliver before going dark, then beginning again with another thin crescent that grows and waxes back to full. Using the cycle is thought to guide and enhance magical practice by matching the energy of the waxing and waning cycles, as well as the full or new moon.

The Dark moon, or witches new moon, is the time between the smallest crescent slivers, at the moon's zero illumination.

July 30

Le Langage de Fleurs was written in 1819 by Madame Charlotte de Latour, pseudonym of Lousie Cortambert. A dictionary of floriography, it contains nearly 300 symbolic meanings of flowers as well as plant uses and history for each. Floral symbology occurs all around the world and has since ancient times. Explore which flowers hold memories or associations for you.

What flower would you choose as a magical symbol?

July 31

Your inner fire requires tending. Self-care, self-awareness, nutrition, movement, and learning provide fuel for passion. Passion drives magic. Passion changes the world. And passion enacted requires energy. Sometimes exhaustion dampens our enthusiasm for things we love. Beyond rest we must take small workable steps to restore ourselves.

Make a summer playlist. Songs about fire or that just increase your vibe! Deep breaths and dancing encouraged.

August

August sees the first of the harvest and the first small hints of change, but there is a slowness to the days as summer lingers. It offers time to stand in the fullness of your life, acknowledge your sovereignty, and know your own worth. You are the child of a thousand generations. In you is an ancient lineage. How you embody your chance here will be your legacy.

August 1

Lughnasa is a Gaelic word meaning August and a festival named for the sun god Lugh. It is the first of three harvest festivals, the other two falling on the equinox in September, and Samhain at the end of October. It is celebrated with fire and dancing and with bread baking and offerings of grain and fruits. Breads are sometimes braided or decorated or made into shapes. Corn husks or sheaves of grain are tied together into dollies, ancient pagan folk sculptures for luck and abundance.

Make a corn dollie from natural materials. Dance around a fire.

August 2

Days are shortening and perhaps you feel summer waning in the cooler weather or the afternoon shadows. Maybe you notice it as people subtly make the mental shift back to structure and goals from downtime and pleasure. Is there any self-work, unfinished business, or seasonal adventure that needs your attention? Attending to whatever it is now will leave you clear for new and exciting experiences in the fall.

Make two lists. One of your favorite moments of summer. The second listing things you would like to experience in the coming fall.

August 3

The Earth element symbolizes stability, ground-edness and physicality. Earth Witches work their magic for a healthy planet- people, animals and nature included. Nesting and hearth spells usually include an earthy component, such as bare feet in the dirt, sand, or grass can be a channel for the element's energy. When in doubt, seek grounding in nature. Walk lightly and connect.

Terrariums, crystals, and natural accents can create an indoor connection with the earth element.

August 4

Using our energy and magic efficiently means understanding what we cannot change, like change itself. As with all of nature, there will be seasons in each life. We will experience a range of circumstances, emotions, and understandings. Joy and sorrow will exist side by side. Time will pass. We must allow for the course of life and stay present.

Fear and regret do not fix or prevent anything.

August 5

A wortcunner is a word that combines the word for 'root' or 'herb' with the word meaning 'to know'. Wise women and Cunning men knew much more than the medicinal uses for plants. They claimed experiences of the deep mysteries, and of learning the secrets of each by speaking directly to the spirit of plants. Magical correspondences and associations have been added to spell work and ritual for millennia and continue today.

Immerse yourself in the deep mysteries of nature and claim their knowledge for yourself.

August 6

Transforming emotion can be a potent source of energy that is often overlooked. Not everything we feel feels good. But it can be used. Anger, hurt, and even grief can be turned to energy if you choose. Burn anger as fuel in a physical way and work your body. Find beauty and knowledge to soothe the mind and soul. Hold space for yourself.

**Alchemy of change—turning
negative or painful emotions
into gold—requires your will,
actions, and awareness.**

August 7

The Latin per fumus means through the smoke. Formulas for perfume were recorded six thousand years ago on clay tablets, and perfumes and incense were integral to the burial rituals in ancient Egypt. They existed in the Indus civilization, and a perfumery was discovered in Pyrgos, Cyprus was dated to more than 4000 years old. Perfume has always been associated with the magical and mystical including glamour magic, attraction spells, charms and pomanders.

Use incense in cleansing or energizing your spaces. Pass through the smoke to receive the energy.

August 8

Self-sabotaging behavior can be as simple as pro-crastination and patterns designed to stop change and keep you in your comfort zone, or it can be more self-destructive choices. A self-sabotaging individual can get overcome by low self-esteem, imposter syndrome or fear of expectations, often driven by negative self-talk. Fear of success and added responsibilities, or pressures of fear of failure or lack of ability can cause the brain to attempt to avoid unpleasantness.

Confront the fear. Once you see it you can beat it.

August 9

The earliest documents mentioning Oxymel come from ancient Greece but the combination syrup of vinegar and honey has likely been used medicinally for much longer. On its own or combined with herbs it was used as specific medicine or as a general tonic. In the 1970s herbalist Rosemary Gladstar popularized the Fire Cider oxymel and it is still a favorite herbal remedy today, often with local variations of ingredients.

Both honey and vinegar have proven pharmacological effects, and oxymels show promise in both the critically and chronically ill.

August 10

You must allow yourself time and space to dream and envision your life. Then you must take the inspired actions to realize and experience your dreams. We are here for a purpose and our dreams will guide us when we are willing and courageous enough to follow them. Whether you create a private sanctuary or solo hike to a mountaintop you need to find the conditions to hear your inner voice. Once you spend time with your core authenticity your choices gain clarity.

Make listening dates with yourself to stay in touch with your voice. It gets louder with practice.

August 11

Today let the hand of love and compassion touch your heart. May kindness surround you, uplift your spirits and fill your soul with warmth. Remember, you deserve to be treated with nothing less than genuine care and understanding. Embrace the beauty of empathy, and let it guide you towards joy and happiness.

Place your hand on your heart. Take a deep breath, calling in light and love. Exhale and let that love and light move into the world again.

August 12

A critical part of embracing your sovereignty is having the capacity to stand or fly alone. Alone with your actions, your visions, your heart, your soul, and your choices. Alone with your Source. It takes courage to go your own way. It may bring situations or relationships to a crossroads, but it will also bring new vistas and opportunities. Do not live a whole life hiding most of yourself away. Anything lost by being yourself will make room for the right things for you.

You don't require anyone or anything to validate who you truly are.

August 13

Casting is divination using small objects such as rocks, crystals, sticks, bones, bits of wood, runes, or dice. Their placement and proximity after the throw is interpreted and assigned meaning. Charm casting is the use of small items of personal significance to do the same thing. Miniature animals, a bit of ribbon, or a key are just a few of countless objects that could be used to represent something specific to you. These are often cast on a pre-marked board, sections assigned meaning as well.

> **Charm items on life boards can be consciously placed to manifest rather than divine.**

August 14

In the fairytale of the frog and the princess, the frog rescues a golden ball she dropped in a pond in exchange for a kiss which breaks the spell and transforms him back to a human prince. Earlier versions have the girl refusing the idea and throwing the frog against a wall which breaks the spell. The concept of kissing many frogs before you find a prince is modern language for persisting until you get your desires.

**A frog amulet or charm can
remind you to persist in pursuit
of the golden ball.**

August 15

In Mesopotamia Sumerians listed hundreds of medicinal herbs on clay tablets. In Ancient China Shen Nong Ben Cao Ling, or The Divine Farmers Classic gathered information on 365 plants and their medicinal uses. The Egyptian Papyrus Ebers contains information on more than 850 plants as well as diseases and treatments. The Sushruta Samhita dates from the 6th Century BCE and describes 700 plant medicines as well as important surgical information.

Otzi the Iceman, frozen in the Alps for five thousand years, carried medicinal plants in his pouch.

August 16

Understanding yourself opens the doors to self-acceptance and self-love, empowering you to embrace your unique qualities and embrace the journey of personal growth. You'll find the courage to break free from limiting beliefs and conditioning to step forward into your authentic power. Knowing what motivates or impedes you gives you the option to change course and create your most authentic existence.

The more you know yourself the more you can grow yourself.

August 17

August 1612 began one of the most well documented witch trials in English history. Thomas Potts, clerk of the court, released an official publication titled The Wonderful Discoverie of Witches in the Countie of Lancaster. When examined in the modern era, witchcraft trials and their associated hysteria involve corruption, revenge, control, and lust for money and power.

They didn't execute witches. They executed women and men.

Witch has been a term used to shame and kill but can be reclaimed as a title of natural power and autonomy. Superstition be damned.

August 18

Rose hips, also called fruit of the rose, form after the rose petals fall away. The round bulb that forms beneath is filled with seeds. Used for centuries for inflammation and pain, rose hips are high in vitamin C. They are made into tea, jams, syrups, or incorporated into cooking. Magically they are linked to love, money, and luck.

Rosehip oil has benefits for skin and wound healing. Rosehip powder is being studied for a multitude of medicinal purposes.

August 19

There is more to the world than can be perceived by human senses, and animals have sensory skills that humans don't have. Fish, frogs, turtles, bees, birds, foxes and dolphins sense the earth's magnetic field.

Other creatures use echolocation, infrared or polarized vision. Electroreception is used by sharks and rays but also bees and platypuses. More animal abilities are being discovered by science every day.

There is a whole universe around us we cannot perceive. That makes it no less real.

August 20

Strong focus comes from both the brain and the mind and is necessary for manifesting, achieving, and magic. The sharper the mind the sharper the intent. The healthier the brain the less distracted and mercurial its functions are. Improving focus means feeding healthy things in each and training your attention to match your intention.

**When is your attention, focus,
and inspiration most aligned?**

August 21

In times of hate, loving the world is a Magical rebellion. Fill the world with grace and compassion using magic in the form of energy and creativity. Hold a light in the darkness and encourage others to hold a light as well. Kindness, compassion, and empathy are superpowers, and readily available for use.

Be an agent of Magical rebellion.

August 22

The Firebird ballet was first performed in Paris in 1910. Composed by Igor Stravinsky and based on the Slavic fairytale it was an immediate success. The legendary bird is described as having brilliant or golden plumage and crystal or glowing eyes. It could bring a blessing or be a harbinger of doom.

What fairytale or legendary creatures do you remember from childhood stories?

August 23

Göbekli Tepe in Turkey is at least eleven thousand years old making it the oldest known temple. Twenty stone circles were discovered with work ongoing to reveal more of them. Massive carved pillars depict animals and symbols. Pillar 43 is called the Vulture Stone and researchers believe it represents a cataclysmic comet strike that caused the sudden cooling of the earth that lasted 1000 years. Sister sites have been discovered nearby but remain unexcavated.

**You are ancient and mysterious.
Excavate what lies under your
surface to find magic and wisdom
that already belongs to you.**

August 24

Even when you have felt like you stumbled, made mistakes, or caused harm to yourself or others, the truth remains: you were always striving to do your best with the knowledge and resources you had at that time. Do not hold on to lingering regrets.

The past doesn't define you nor should it hold you back from embracing the joys of the present and the endless possibilities of the future.

Forgive yourself. There's joyous work to do.

August 25

The I-Ching, sometimes translated as Book of Changes, is a Chinese text of divination that is over 3000 years old. Lengths of yarrow stalks were manipulated to produce numbers which were then interpreted from written lines in the book. Yarrow was used in divining love in European practices, and Victorians used it to symbolize lasting love. It was a sacred herb to Druids who used it to divine weather.

**Yarrow is loved by pollinators
and is a hardy and nearly
carefree perennial.**

August 26

Sailing well requires trimming your sails to make maximum use of the winds and their energy. In each of our lives we have challenges and abilities, deficits and skills. How aware we are of the direction of energy flow in our lives added to our skill set and knowledge determines where and how well we sail. Hoist your sails and set out on adventure.

The world is your ocean.

August 27

The words Always and Never can be powerful and especially when misapplied. When we use these words to describe our attitude, mindset, tastes and views we can self-define right into a corner. Leave room in your life for growth and discovery. We are not meant to congeal into some final form with all our opinions set. We are supposed to exist in wonder and awe at the magic of being here at all.

Don't limit yourself or your experiences by over defining yourself.

August 28

Indigenous North American tribes grew Sunflowers almost 5000 years ago, using the seeds and oil in a multitude of ways. The Aztecs used them in the Temple of the Sun. The head of the sunflower is made up of tiny flowers, each producing a seed. The spirals of the seeds follow the Fibonacci Sequence.

They symbolize the energy and vibrance of the sun, loyalty, friendship, and happiness.

**Use sunflowers and their
seeds in your rituals, spells,
or meditation.**

August 29

Become a collector of good people. Notice those around you who are supportive of others, helpful, kind, and open. People who want to make things better, starting with themselves. When you find those people let them know they are seen and appreciated. The synergy of collaboration and cooperation expands our collective possibilities.

Attract good people by being one.

August 30

The Luna moth, or Moon moth, only lives about a week after emerging from its cocoon and never eats. They are beautiful and mysterious and are variously seen as messengers from the afterlife and as harbingers of luck and wealth. With a wingspan of more than four inches it is one of the largest moths in North America.

Luna moths symbolize metamorphosis, heightened perception, and intuition.

August 31

In this ever-changing world, certainty can be elusive. But you are constantly evolving with every choice you make. The unknown holds endless possibilities. Allow yourself to explore new paths, challenge your beliefs, and uncover the depths of your being. Each moment is a chance to recreate yourself and a future that aligns with your core. Be willing to venture into the realm of uncertainty. Gifts and understanding can be found there.

Trust the process. Trust yourself.
Answers will come.

The Autumn Witch

The Autumn Witch is the wildest witch, for she has come full circle to her power and is living in wholeness and authenticity. She has come home to herself. Her magic is Harvest and Gratitude and Abundance. The magic of connection and completion. She loves the morning mist and golden afternoons, savoring and thriving in the wild stir of autumn. She celebrates the moment and allows her senses to keep her present amid the mystical pull of magic, moonlight, and memory. And she lets her heart fly

Embrace and Celebrate Autumn Magic

- Plant a tree or plant spring bulbs.
- Discover and honor ancestors.
- Bake and make soup.
- Find a pocket charm to fit your intentions.
- Create a gratitude altar.
- Walk in the crisp air.
- Have a bonfire.

Symbols, Scents, & Such

Apples, Pumpkins

Acorns, woodsmoke

Falling leaves

Cornucopia

Red, orange, yellow

Crows, ravens, bats, cats

Cider

September

Like the turn of every season, September is a beginning and an ending. The days grow increasingly shorter, and the strength of the sun noticeably lessens. Focus shifts from the play of summer back to purposeful learning. We gather the knowledge and tools to see us through the coming dark half of the year. The equinox brings us to the halfway point between solstices, allowing a moment to stop and consider what we desire to create and what we wish to leave behind. Autumn is a season when shadows grow long, and magic seems to rise.

September 1

Meteorological fall can bring a mix of feelings as summer passes and autumn brings its changes. Take some time to consider what you want from the coming season. Set intentions or add to your skill set. Consider what you have experienced this year, and what the harvest was from the places you invested your time and energy. Count your blessings.

Make a gratitude jar to collect slips of paper you write over the next weeks naming all that you are grateful for. Read them to yourself on Thanksgiving or in a personal ritual.

September 2

Look for joy. Allow the small moments to fill you with the things you need like love, hope, or confidence. It is easy to let the world and all of its information and confusion overwhelm our capacity to stop and smell the roses. It is in the small moments of witnessing beauty or compassion that we can ground and balance. Let simple things sink deeply into your heart, and moments of goodness stretch your capacity to hold it.

Imagine holding joy as a tiny spark in your hand, and the more present you are to the wonder around you, the brighter it glows.

September 3

Wild apples were cultivated by Neolithic farmers 8,000 years ago. The ancient Egyptians grew them in the Nile Delta. The ancient Romans planted orchards in Britain. Everywhere the apple has grown it has been entwined in folklore and ritual. From the Garden of Eden to the Garden of Hesperides to the Isle of Avalon, mystical stories surround the apple.

**Go apple picking or cook with
fresh apples for kitchen witchery.
Explore folktale and myth to
learn more about the magical
associations of apples.**

September 4

Western magical traditions recognize earth, air, fire, and water as the elements, but Eastern traditions include metal. A symbol of wisdom, justice, and strength, it is associated with the energy of the feminine Divine, or yin. In Chinese medicine metal is the element associated with confidence, intuition, and the ability to let go.

A coin, charm, or piece of jewelry can be used as a reminder to practice the art of letting go.

September 5

Learning new skills grows your confidence, your abilities, and your possibilities. Gathering new knowledge can be a part of a larger manifestation ritual. Applying action and energy enables the desired outcome. A new language can be learned for travel wishes or endurance training will prepare you to climb a mountain. Bring body, mind, and spirit into your quest.

Give yourself the skills and knowledge to reach for your dreams.

September 6

The Malleus Maleficarum, also known as The Hammer of Witches, was written in 1486 by Heinrich Kramer. Angered and shamed by a failed persecution of witches in Innsbruck he wrote the treatise for inquisitors, prosecutors, and clergymen to more efficiently persecute women accused of witchcraft. His methods included deceit and torture to extract confessions. Prior to his work simple witchcraft was punishable by time spent in the stocks. Kramer encouraged the same punishment as for heretics, burning alive at the stake.

Translations of this work are available online, in libraries, and in bookstores.

September

September 7

The Silk Road was a network of ancient overland and sea trades routes that connected the Orient to the Mediterranean and Africa. Goods such as silk, spices, jade and porcelain moved along the routes for 1500 years. Caravansaries were inns built along the way that catered to caravans of traders and travelers. Knowledge, politics, religion, and diversity of experience led to the founding of culturally blended towns and cities.

**Imagine an oasis of diversity,
acceptance, and shared knowledge.**

September 8

To pause and to hesitate are not the same. Pause is not an action of doubt. It is an intentional, thoughtful gathering of your power before moving forward. Hesitation is a stoppage of energy, a withdrawal of surety that indicates fear. Boldness is required to face chaos with confidence, to grasp the moment with intent and not be paralyzed into non-action.

You are the pause in the chaos. Everything whirling is a potential tool or opportunity. You got this.

September 9

Crows are highly intelligent, can complete complex tasks and have long memories. They've been the harbinger of both good and ill luck among different cultures from Native America to Russia and Japan. Dozens of myths and legends incorporate the crow and crow symbolism. To the Celts they were sacred to Morrigan who shapeshifted to a crow as goddess of war and death. Odin had two crow companions.

**Crow symbolism can be a
powerful reminder to use your
wisdom and wits.**

September 10

Cliodna appears in Celtic mythology as a sea goddess, mermaid, and Queen of the Banshees. She represents love, passion, and deep beauty. Legend tells of her three birds who eat apples from an otherworld tree, giving them a song with the ability to heal. She is also known as a shapeshifter, turning herself into a wren, a sea bird, or a large white rabbit. Every ninth wave is sacred to her and can be worked with for granting wishes.

If you could shapeshift, what form would you take?

September 11

The Lacnunga is an Anglo-Saxon collection of works that contain prayers, charms, herbal remedies, and blessings for both animals and people. Compiled about the 10th century it contains versions of older writings. Mostly written in Old English and Latin, there are bits of Greek, Aramaic, Hebrew and Old Irish. Among references to elves, sentient flora and spirits are important documentation of folk medicine and religious beliefs. Most famously it contains a protective prayer charm called the Lorica of Laidcenn and The Nine Herbs Charm.

**Humans have always sought
to understand themselves
and their world.**

September 12

Struggle and obstacles can seem insurmountable, and your own abilities can seem in doubt. Then it is most important to know that you are powerful and capable of overcoming anything. Remember that you've made it through tough times before, and you will again. Believe in yourself and your ability to rise above all challenge. You have what it takes to succeed, even when things seem impossible.

Keep moving forward, and don't give up—your victory is just around the corner.

September 13

Homecoming celebrations are generally held in the autumn when schools and churches welcome back those who once lived among them, and often to memorialize those members lost during the year. Celebrations of games or dancing, dedications of new things, and celebration of milestones are common, and traditional rituals may be observed.

**Homecoming of the self is time
to stop and look at what the year
has brought or taken, and the
friendship and experiences shared.**

September 14

Resilience is not just bouncing back; it's about adapting and evolving in the face of the change. Remember that you have an incredible capacity to be flexible, to solve old problems and new challenges using what you have learned. Lacking resilience is a kind of brittleness, too easily broken. Be flexible in your mindset, actions, and reactions and watch as you navigate through life with more grace and determination.

**Let your resilience shape
your journey.**

September 15

Songbirds, shorebirds and all manner of waterfowl are beginning their return migration, called by instinct. They navigate using the earth's electro-magnetic field, position of the sun and stars, and even smell, but the exact means and mechanism to their abilities isn't fully known, but that doesn't stop the magic from happening.

**Embrace the mystery and magic
in the universe.**

September 16

In the Middle Ages the Tempestarii were feared magicians, believed to be able to control the weather. Witches too were said to be able to raise storms that could destroy crops or sink ships. King James of Scotland, commissioner of the KJV Bible, was obsessed with witches, believing they had conjured a storm to kill him crossing the North Sea, and large numbers were plotting his defeat. He sanctioned torture and murder of human beings for superstitious fear. In 2022 the Scottish government and Church of Scotland apologized for their deaths.

Superstition is destructive. Holy does not harm.

September 17

Life is a journey of self-discovery, and it's normal to be a mystery even to yourself. Certainty can be elusive. But the beauty of it is that you are constantly evolving with every choice along the way. Each moment is a chance to redefine and create a future that aligns with your desires. Don't be afraid to venture into the realm of uncertainty. Take one step and then look around and decide for yourself.

Embrace the unknown, for it holds endless possibilities.

September 18

Lighthouse Magic can be both a core magic and a situational magic. All humans contain the light of the stars and other celestial beings. When you shine your light as a beacon for others, ensure you are grounded on your shore of authenticity first. You do not go out to others, rather you stand your ground and provide a strong signal that others can follow to secure and safe harbor. Look for others in your circle who practice lighthouse magic, for they can support you when you are being tossed on wild seas and have temporarily lost your way.

Lighthouses provide the world with access to portals unimagined.

September 19

Nearing the equinox we move from the physical toward our spirit. Harvest season teaches us to really see our blessings and embrace gratitude, even as we enter the dark half of the year. Journaling, memoir, and handwritten letters are a few ways to capture the moments and the gifts.

Encourage and strengthen your spirit by reading and writing beautiful words.

September 20

Body painting and tattooing are part of cultural and magical practice worldwide. Tattooing existed among nearly all ancient cultures and had a range of uses, even marking slaves, criminals, and spies. They were used in rituals, magical protection, and memorializing the dead, clan affiliation and more from the South Pacific to the Arctic to Africa. Body painting might be used short term for ceremonies of magic, religion or as a life phase initiation. Worn daily, such as cosmetics, it was used to delineate status and wealth.

**Henna tattoos can be an artistic
and spiritual experience.**

September 21

The Autumnal equinox is the midpoint between summer and winter and is celebrated most often as a harvest festival. Often seen as a point of balance, equinoxes have been observed around the world for many ages. Ancient megaliths aligned to the sun on equinoxes include Chichén-Itzá pyramid in Mexico, the Ring of Brodgar in Scotland, Intihuatana Stone in Peru, and the Great Sphinx in Egypt. Celebration of the equinox has many names and traditions and connects us to our ancient rhythms and cycles.

With these ancient observances in mind, create your own tradition or celebration.

September 22

There are many origin stories about Thieves oil. In the early 1400s the Bubonic Plague, known as the Black Death, was raging. A story recorded in the Royal English Archives tells of four thieves who used a blend of oils to protect from the contagion allowing them to rob the dead. When caught they gave the recipe to the King in exchange for not burning at the stake. The blend of essential oils most often includes cinnamon, lemon, rosemary, clove, and eucalyptus.

Herbal oils are being studied and used medicinally even today.

September 23

Gratitude is energy in motion, vibrating at a frequency that attracts abundance. Be grateful and appreciate all that you have and all of the circumstances in your life, even as you intend and invite a better future. Attune yourself to the magical force of gratitude and it will invoke a cycle of abundance in your life.

**Create a morning or evening
ritual of counting blessings
and receiving.**

September 24

Soup is a fun way to enjoy the autumn season and use a bit of kitchen magic. From your recipe to your selection of ingredients to the cooking and stirring it all together, soup is a chance to brew up a pot of magical goodness. For celebrating the season shift, or healing, or even to dish up some love. Consider your intention clearly as you work.

Discover a cookbook of witchy recipes or create your own.

September 25

Bats are fascinating and misunderstood night-flying creatures whose symbolism varies across cultures. The Puritans feared them because they believed humans could be bewitched by them. Mayans revered them as rulers of the night. Chinese culture holds them as symbols of happiness and fortune. Western folklore and classical literature tie the bat to vampires, and the witches in Macbeth used them in a spell.

Bats use echolocation to navigate and hunt, making sounds above the range of human hearing.

September 26

Autumn and winter offer a chance to draw your energy in and downward and begin to explore the depths of yourself. Consider all that makes you who you are. Do your actions and priorities align? Are you caring for yourself? Have you abandoned any parts of yourself? Asking yourself questions and answering honestly can bring mental and emotional clarity.

Tell yourself the unvarnished truth.

September 27

Mushrooms are food, medicine, and poison. In Ancient Egypt only the nobility could even touch them, considered food of the Gods. Greek soldiers ate them for strength in battle. As medicine, they were used all over the world. The hallucinogenic properties of some species have found their way into ritual, recreation and religion. Many species are highly toxic. Examples of misuse exist throughout history. Nutritional and medicinal use research continues today, revealing the amazing properties of these fungi.

**Mushrooms symbolize
enlightenment and emergence
from darkness.**

September 28

Autumn brings the falling leaves, a beautiful visual reminder of transition and cycles of the seasons. The trees draw the sap from the leaves, drawing down to their roots only that which will nourish and sustain them. The bond where the leaf attaches weakens, and eventually the wind carries it away. Leaf symbolism can be used for spells or rituals, especially for release.

**Catch a falling leaf. Make an
autumn wish.**

September 29

The oldest discovered musical instrument in the world is the Neanderthal flute, possibly sixty thousand years old. It was found in a cave above the Idrijca River in Slovenia in the area around a hearth. It was made from the thigh bone of a cave bear. Music has been a part of human life since the beginning. The archeological records show varied carved flutes, percussion, and eventually stringed instruments. Rock art in France dated to 13,000 years ago depicts a sorcerer playing a bow or a flute.

Music is a magical language.

September 30

Luna was a Roman goddess of heaven and the full moon, feminine energy, childbirth and agriculture. She could bestow visions and is associated with intuition. She was believed to bring solutions through dreams, when the mind is ready to receive guidance. Often depicted with long dark hair and pale skin, she drives a silver chariot pulled by oxen, horses or dragons.

**Invite Luna to open your mind
to solutions in a bedtime ritual
of envisioning the moon.**

October

October is perhaps the time most associated with magic and is often referred to as the Season of the witch, and there is no better time to claim your title. It brings the harvest moon and the Celtic festival of Samhain, when the veil between worlds is thinnest. It is also the Celtic New Year, the end of harvest, and considered the beginning of winter. October weather can be warm and golden, or misty and moody, beautiful in all of its aspects. Just like you. Let October work its spell on you.

October 1

Autumn is synonymous to the season of the witch. The mists and moonrises of October seem to hold extra mystery and magic. As you move through these darkening days consider how you are using your magic, or if you are on autopilot. Look for places in your daily routine to add consciousness and attention. Personalize your care rituals. Make room for introspection and consider your intentions for the dark half of the year. Make sure you know what it is you want. Then take action. Give it your energy and focus. Step forward.

**You are a magical creature.
Walk like one.**

October 2

Harps are ancient instruments and legends abound of their power and mystery. Folklore, fairy tales, songs and poetry tell of their use for an assortment of magical needs from healing to enchantment. Celtic bards and Russian guslars were formally educated in the creation and use poetic language and music. Harp spells were used for protection, success in battle, and even to ease childbirth.

**Harp music can accompany
any magical practice,
listening or playing.**

October 3

Pumpkins are most often associated with pies and jack-o-lanterns. Cultivated in the Americas for thousands of years, they are packed with nutrition and store well. A symbol of harvest and abundance they can be easily incorporated into a seasonal practice to remind you to draw on and use the energy of Autumn.

Use pumpkins to decorate or cook. Make a seasonal altar of gratitude, create a new recipe, or find an old one.

October 4

Familiar fall spices include cinnamon, nutmeg, ginger, clove, and allspice. Each of these carries a long history of magical, religious, and medicinal use. Though ancient and sacred, modern society knows the blend as pumpkin spice. Blended together or used separately, autumn spices evoke the season with exciting taste and scent. Warm and comforting they bring memories of celebrations and seasons past.

Potpourri, scented besoms, and simmer pots are simple ways to use spices in everyday magic.

October 5

Oaks and acorns have sacred meanings for many cultures and feature in their lore and myth. The Druids worshiped in oak groves and in Norse mythology oak is associated with Thor. Oaks grow tall and attract lightning but continue to thrive when struck. Strength, power, perseverance, and patience are all contained in the acorn.

Carrying an acorn or wearing a charm can help connect you to the strength you already possess.

October 6

Cider is a drink made from the expressed juice of apples. To produce hard cider the juice is put through a fermentation process. Pomona, Roman goddess of orchards and fruit trees was said to not only care for the trees but made a magic elixir from the juice of the apples. A symbol of abundance and the harvest, cider, sweet or hard, is perfect for seasonal celebration.

Toasting can become expressions of gratitude, wishmaking, or remembrance of ancestors.

October 7

The day you were born is a day to be celebrated. It marks the beginning of your holy Soul becoming the sovereign being you are meant to be. Your purpose is unique. There may be many distractions along your life journey. Some of them will be fun and exciting; others dark and untenable. Know that no moment of your life has been wasted. Even when you cannot see the purpose of your experiences, each one is moving you in the direction of your destiny.

Remember who you are. Be conscious and aware in every moment and you will live a magical life.

October 8

Fairytales are much more than entertaining stories. They teach about the range of human experiences and emotions, overcoming obstacles and challenges, belief in oneself, and good and evil. The oldest known fairytale, about a smith who trades his soul to the devil for magical powers, dates from the Bronze age, roughly six thousand years ago.

What challenge or obstacle in your life could you write as a fairytale, and what is the moral?

October 9

The symbol of the hourglass denotes the finite, the cycles of life, endings, and when reversed it brings new beginnings. Every turn of the glass our lives are changing, and the challenges and possibilities are new. It asks the question of how you will spend this time. In ritual or craft an hourglass might be used to hold a focus or meditation, aid a spellcasting or breath work. It can become a tool for dedicated time for learning or physical activity.

Tempus Fugit.

October 10

When separating wheat from chaff, keep what is useful and life sustaining from what is empty and unwanted. Winnow means to blow and let the wind flow through, take away what isn't needed. What in your life is no longer sustaining or serving you? What is good and nourishing and should be kept?

Stand in the wind and imagine it blowing through your body, your heart, and your mind. Visualize the chaff lifting away into the autumn air.

October 11

A woman aligned with her power and willing to use it always risks being called unpleasant names. What others can't understand or control they must degrade. It isn't your job to correct them, just keep making your choices and moves. Every rock that gets thrown at you can be used to build your castle on, but you can't let people into your head, or manipulate your emotions, or drain you until you quit.

I am a Woman Inspiring Tolerance, Compassion, and Humanity.

October 12

Checking in with your body frequently and responding to what it needs will not only show you opportunities to improve your well-being, but strengthen the connection between mind, body, and brain. A scanning meditation flowing from head to feet allows you to feel any place you are holding tightness and begin to release it.

Let yourself get used to being in your body and aware. Practice often to become familiar where you hold stress and blocks.

October 13

Deciding to be your own best friend is a beautiful gift that allows you to love yourself unconditionally, trust your intuition, and practice self-care. You become your own support system and cheerleader, always there to lift yourself up and celebrate your victories. As your own best friend, you allow other relationships to come from joy as opposed to need.

**Befriending yourself sends
a message to the women and
girls in your life, allowing
them to do the same.**

October 14

Fog and mist have a magic even today in the way it moves us with presence or promise. It is no surprise it acquired several mystical associations over time. Sometimes believed to be a thinning place that creates a passageway between the worlds of physical and spiritual, fog enchants with its ephemeral beauty.

Modern craft practices using fog include transformative manifestation, seeking answers from within, or setting a tone for a charm or spell. Reversed it can be used to hide, confuse, or deceive.

October 15

It took a great many people to get you here. Beyond your parents, there were four grandparents, and eight great grandparents, and so on. Doubling at each generation the numbers quickly rise as you move backwards through time, and all of those individuals contributed to the existence you have now. Consider all the love, hard work, loss, laughter and amazing things seen.

**You are a living legacy, connecting
the past to the future.**

October 16

While we should be present and mindful of the current moment, feelings, memories, aspirations, and hopes need addressing. Writing letters to the past and future can clear space in your head, and help you to think in new, helpful ways about who you are. The past can't be changed, but we change as we grow and begin to look at old things with a fresh perspective and release what doesn't serve. The future you want can't be created until you know what you want. Write it down.

Burning both letters can be a ritual to release both regret and expectation, inviting a flow state.

October 17

Autumn is an opportunity to practice your sensory skills. Colors, smells, tastes, textures and sounds are all around. Pick one or two senses to concentrate on becoming aware of as you go through the season or make a practice of trying to notice something every day from each sensory category. Pay attention to your body as you experience them to strengthen your practice, connection, and intuition.

Let your senses do their job of teaching you about the world and your body.

October 18

Imagination and intuition are two amazing traits that can lead you down pathways you never thought possible, tapping into the magic and power you have as a divine human. So, why not step outside the rigidity of your rational mind, into your superpower and use your own imagination to create endless possibilities today?

**Embrace the magic within you
and the full power of creative
thought, and the flow will
astound you.**

October 19

The Mid-Autumn Festival is an important holiday in Chinese culture that dates back more than 3000 years. Families and friends gather to give thanks for the harvest, offering gratitude and prayers. Celebrated with lanterns and mooncakes, it venerates the moon goddess Chang'e. She is often depicted floating toward the moon along with her pet Yu Tu, the moon rabbit.

**The autumn full moon is
symbolic of abundance, luck,
and harmony.**

October 20

When we do not live consciously, with awareness and presence, we slip into a type of a default setting. It may feel soothing as an anodyne to stress or trauma, but numbness comes at a cost. Not only can't we process what we feel, we lose our ability to act on our own behalf. It may seem easier to let life make the choices for you, but it will never help you embody your power.

**Living consciously allows for the
full range of experience of and
interaction with your own life.**

October 21

Our choices send messages to our body. It is never about just cutting out the negatives, it is about embracing the good. Send your body the message that you care about its wellbeing and needs. Be careful of sending messages of deprivation and resistance. Learn how your brain and body work, and what they require. Stop looking at exercise or healthy eating as punishment. Find healthy choices you enjoy.

**Celebrate having the gift of a
body by supporting it.**

October 22

Diana is the Roman goddess of the hunt, nature, and animals and is often depicted with a bow and arrows. She is also a fertility goddess associated with conception and childbirth, and the moon. The twin sister of Apollo, she is symbolized by the crescent moon, which sometimes forms her bow. She is a virgin in the ancient meaning, an autonomous woman, a woman of agency.

Dianic Wicca is a modern goddess tradition focused on feminine empowerment.

October 23

Negative body image can cause mood and eating disorders, low self-esteem, social anxieties and can affect many aspects of quality of life. Young girls are particularly vulnerable, but it can impact a woman at any life stage. Body image is perception, thoughts and feelings that are both conscious and unconscious. Distortion can come from media, advertising, and social pressure, but can also stem from relatives and friends.

**Develop compassion and
acceptance for yourself. Accept
that you are unique and beautiful.
Help others do the same.**

October 24

Spiders are a powerful symbol in many cultures. In some creation stories it is the Spider who weaves the world into being, and there are many spider gods and goddesses to be found among the Greek, African, Native American, Egyptian, and Asian legends. Often associated with weaving and spinning and divine feminine, some cultures attribute the origin of weaving, net making and knotwork to the spider's example.

**Spider charms and symbolism
can be used magically to invoke
feminine energy.**

October 25

Joy is not simply a feeling of happiness. It is an attitude and a choice, just like love. Holding on to painful experiences, judging the world through the lens of anger and bitterness disallows the experience of joy. In a balanced approach to life, it must be acknowledged that joy and sorrow coexist. We cannot avoid unpleasantness in life, or dodge all the pain, but between the storms we must embrace the beauty that life offers while we can.

**Be careful not to separate
yourself from joy.**

October 26

Rhiannon is a Welsh goddess of the underworld
and very ancient. She may have been the original
Mother goddess of the Celts. Her name means
divine or great queen. She brings comfort in hard
times, bestowing the gifts of tears and forgetful-
ness, but she is also a goddess of movement, magic,
and transformative change. She sends restorative
sleep and dreams to guide us, and even nightmares
to get our attention.

**Tears from emotion are called
psychogenic. They differ chemically
from irritation and maintenance
tears, and provide release of
hormones and brain chemicals.**

October 27

Cats were sacred in Ancient Egypt and appear in art and mummified remains. Even older evidence of the connection between humans and felines come from a grave discovered in Cyprus. Dated at 9500 years old the grave contained a human next to a large cat and multiple grave goods. Cats across time have had many mythical and magical associations, with black cats becoming associated with witches and demons. Witches were said to be able to shapeshift into feline form.

Visualize shifting into a cat. What adventures would you have?

October 28

While carving faces into vegetables occurs in many cultures, the idea of doing so at Halloween is tied to the legend of Jack O'Lantern, known as Stingy Jack. After tricking the Devil twice, and being shut out of heaven for his behavior, he was given a glowing ember to see by and left to walk the night. He carved a turnip to set it in and has roamed the earth since. In January 1836 the Dublin Penny Journal published the legend, and immigrants to America brought the folk tale with them, finding pumpkins to be excellent for carving. They are still a part of Halloween celebrations today.

Carve a Jack O'Lantern.

October 29

What makes a woman a witch? That is unique to each woman who embraces her magic, but there are commonalities. A Wild and Wise Witch believes in herself and believes she makes a difference. She can consciously make herself stronger and smarter. She accepts the fullness of life, knows joy and sorrow are part of living. She can envision and dream change into reality. She manifests her desires.

A witch is someone who makes magic with their life.

October 30

There are strategies and techniques you can use to build your self-trust and confidence. One technique is to set small, achievable goals for yourself and work towards them. Building a sense of accomplishment and progress boosts your self-esteem. Another strategy is practicing self-care and maintaining good physical and mental health. This includes getting enough sleep, exercising regularly, and eating a healthy diet. Surround yourself with supportive people who encourage and believe in you.

Challenge negative self-talk.
Replace it with words that will
benefit and strengthen you.

October 31

In the 8th century the Catholic Church changed the date of All Saints' Day, overlapping All Hallowtide with the Celtic observance of Samhain, the beginning of the dark half of the year. Ancient Celts would set a place at the table and beside the fire for their loved ones. Livestock were driven between ritual bonfires to cleanse them, and divination was practiced using apples or nuts. The veil to the otherworld was thought to thin, and there was danger from wandering spirits or fairies. Mumming and guising are protective.

Open your intuitive sense to the seasonal magic and feel the unseen around you.

November

November brings your journey full circle. You can bear witness to the cycle of death and rebirth and the power contained in each process. It is a month of gratitude for the whole of life, for our experiences, and the love connections we make. It takes us to a deeper, quieter place, where we can see clearly and choose our way forward. November calls us close to the fire, calls us home to our truest selves. Embrace your power to affect your world. Know it as your own, and do not fear it. Let it flow out from you. Carry the light into the dark. The world needs you now.

November 1

Dia de los Muertos is a Latin American holiday to celebrate and remember the dead. Observed at the beginning of November the day is a Combination of Aztec beliefs and religious culture brought by the Spanish invasion. Altars are decorated with candles, food, and items representative of relatives who have passed so that spirits can find their way back. Graveyards are cleaned and decorated, and families have picnic feasts. Children are presented to their ancestors and songs are sung.

Skeletons are symbols of humanness, a reminder that death is part of life and a passage we all make.

November 2

Hiding your light sometimes feels like the easiest thing to do. We know that if we stand up as our truest self there could be a backlash and not everyone will like us. The reasons we hide are numerous, but reaching for your own magic also means it is time to reach for the best of yourself. If you are doing your work, making your choices, sharing your gifts and living in authenticity, outside validation becomes moot.

Your worth is determined by you.

November 3

Josephine Dodge founded The National Association Opposed to Women Suffrage, an all women organization with half a million members by 1919. A year later the 19th Amendment would pass, ending a 70-year fight to give women the right to vote. Later the Equal Rights amendment was tracking to become law. In 1972 another woman, Phyllis Schlafly, led a winning campaign against it. Celebrating defeat of the sex discrimination bill, the band played "Ding Dong the Witch is Dead".

**There have been women in
history who have worked
against female autonomy.
There still are today.**

November 4

When you throw a rock into water you can see the ripples go out from the center, the point of impact. The choices we make, and the actions we take, create ripples we can't see. Our words and deeds affect the people and situations around us. When making choices of how to meet our needs and desires or use our will, we must act responsibly and with discernment, but we will always make ripples and that is okay.

**Your job is not to calm the waters,
but to live authentically and fully.**

November 5

In 1428 Joan of Arc was a poor teenager before convincing King Charles of France to let her lead his armies in the ongoing war, saying God had sent her to bring France victory. She cut her hair, put on armor and did just that, standing with the King as he was crowned. Months later she was captured in battle, accused of witchcraft and wearing men's clothes. The church had a purview of miracles and angels. All else was the work of demons, witches, and magic. She burned at the stake in 1431 at age 19. The king did not intervene.

Powerful women have always been feared. Follow your vision.

November 6

Any type of power can cause harm when wielded in ignorance or malice. Destruction requires no talent, no brilliance, no heart. For every action we take there are effects and consequences. We are an active part of creation in our lives and in the world. Power used consciously, with love and brilliance, is the most potent magic of all.

When deciding how to apply our magic or any other power we must use discernment and self-honesty.

November 7

Mysticism is the belief in a direct connection to the ultimate truth or the Divine that can be made through personal experience, knowledge, and connection to wisdom. Fundamentalism relies on strict interpretation of text, dogma, and conformity. One is a path of joy and the other the path of judgment. In theistic mysticism adherents of the major religions have more in common in their beliefs than they do with fundamentalists inside their own religion.

**Nothing stands between
you and Source.**

November 8

Life lessons are meant to set you free from conditioning and judgment, not imprison you. Not every experience that impacts us is gentle and it can be difficult to untangle the beneficial lessons that may be contained within. Resistance to circumstance and processing of associated feelings can be crippling, but sorting through, even a bit at a time, can begin to loosen the constrictions and set us free.

Do the work. Learn from your experience and then use it to live your best authentic life. It's not only possible, it's the path of least resistance.

November 9

Veronica Franco was a Venetian poet and courtesan in the late 1500s. Educated and raised for this purpose, she was listed as a cortigiana onesta, an honest courtesan. Her education would have gone beyond the basics to include instruction in the arts, etiquette, conversation, and more at a time women were not allowed a public education. She gained access to prestigious literary salons and worked with both male and female writers. Known for her philanthropy and proto-feminist views she was called before the Inquisition on charges of witchcraft.

She stood in her own defense and won.

November 10

Many neopagan traditions honor the triple goddess in her aspects of the maiden, the mother, and the crone. The three are representative of the three phases of womanhood and the reproductive cycles the female body passes through. This is often represented in the phases of the moon as waxing, full, then waning. Triple deities can be found in multiple cultures and religions and are reflected in art and myth.

**Use the phases of the moon to honor
all the aspects you contain.**

November 11

This year of practicing with your senses, communicating with your body, developing your intuition, feeding your brain, learning and exploring and knowing yourself has deepened you. You take your awareness and energy and intention with you every day and move forward in an intentional way. Continue to develop your core even as you explore your outer possibilities. Keep reaching deep.

You are well on your way, and you understand the path is yours to walk.

November 12

It is okay to be scared. But you still have to get out there, open up, love fully, make mistakes, learn and become stronger. Courageous women will tell you that they accomplished great things by using their fear to move them forward, and even reach seemingly impossible goals. Fear is energy-in-motion. Use the momentum to do what you know must be done.

**You are capable of bending
fear into flow.**

November 13

In 1937 comic strip L'il Abner ran a story line about a day for women to literally catch a man with marriage as the prize. Just two years later Sadie Hawkins Day celebrations were all the rage on college campuses. Beyond dances, the day represented a change in a time where romantic relationships were to only be initiated by men. A new freedom, of not having to wait to be chosen, presented itself.

**When you accept your freedom
you are limitless.**

November 14

Autumn's mood is one of memory, of times past and sometimes of mistakes made. We go on and grow and change and don't always realize that we have held onto these things in the corners of our hearts and minds. Find time to sit with these old ghosts. Invite all your past selves with acceptance. You can invite them to tell their stories, or just sit in peace with them. When you are ready, send the ones you can into the light.

**Give grace and gratitude to
your other-selves.**

November 15

Even when we have embraced our magic things can happen to make us feel as if we have lost our connection to it. Grief, trauma, illness and addiction are just a few of the ways we can lose ourselves. Know that the problem isn't with your power but with the energy reserves needed to wield it. Sometimes our magic is a tiny ember we must protect, deep inside. Let it settle there. Give yourself care on every level. Breathe, nourish, rest. Nurse yourself as you would a beloved.

Your magic will not leave you.

November 16

Hekate is a Greek goddess of witchcraft, magic, the moon, ghosts, and the creatures of the night. She is often depicted with a torch and is sacred to crossroads and thresholds. Her mythology is ancient and complex, and she had power over heaven and earth, the sea, and the underworld. Her origin is debated with theories that include Egypt, Anatolia, and Greece.

Recognize the places and times thresholds and crossroads appear in your life. Move forward with awareness and intention.

November 17

You can be whole in an incomplete space. You don't have to wait for the perfect set of circumstances, the right job or relationship. Wholeness depends greatly on self-love, and self-knowledge, both within your control. Your life is always yours to claim. Even when circumstances are difficult and feel slow to change, you can quietly commit to yourself.

**Wholeness comes from being
fully present to yourself, with
reverence and grace.**

November 18

Chaos Magic as a movement emerged in 1970s England as an alternative to organized religious magic and hierarchy and drawing on the work of Austin Osman Spare. In Chaos work, belief itself is a tool and a type of psychic energy, and our perceptions create our reality. Magicians themselves create their own systems and practices and apply their own will towards outcomes.

"Magick is the Science of understanding oneself and one's own situation. It is the art of applying this knowledge in action."
Aleister Crowley

November 19

The Vagus nerve is part of your parasympathetic nervous system. It sends signals between your brain and your heart, lungs, and digestive tract. Messages are delivered about the health and safety of your body. This affects mood, immune responses and more. Breath work, humming and singing and even gargling are among ways to tone the nerve.

Strengthen the Vagus nerve to increase health and resilience and reduce anxiety.

November 20

Thanksgiving festivities include family, food, and gratitude. Traditionally it is a time for expressing thanks for the bounty of the harvest of our lives. In modern times and with distance or strains within families the tradition of Friendsgiving has evolved. When practiced fully, gratitude goes beyond a feeling.

Celebrate gratitude in a tangible way. Give back to the world in time, effort, and love.

November 21

Hypatia was born around 350 CE in Alexandria, Egypt. She was a highly regarded mathematician, astronomer, philosopher and teacher. Although she was pagan, her students were largely Christian. She was popular with the people of Alexandria and had some political influence. Then Cyril of Alexandria came to power. He was distrusted by Hypatia and her students. Cyril and his defenders started rumors of satanism and magic. In 415 a Christian mob pulled her from her carriage. They ripped her body apart and burned the pieces.

Decide for yourself. Don't succumb to mob mentality. It is always dangerous.

November 22

Aconite, also known as wolfsbane or monkshood, is one of the deadliest herbs associated with ancient witchcraft. Known as the Queen of Poisons, it takes a very small amount to kill and should never be handled or used in modern craft. Because of its beautiful blueish purple flowers, it is still cultivated in perennial gardens. Legality of growing it can differ by region. Associated with both Hekate and Cerredwin, its roots are often black.

Know what you are working with. Even beautiful things can hide a dark nature.

November 23

Ancient humans mapped the night sky and built huge megalithic structures used to measure time, create agricultural calendars, and aid navigation. Modern research of thirty-thousand-year-old cave paintings suggest depictions of star constellations thousands of years before Ancient Greeks were studying astronomy. Belief that human destiny is written in the stars led to the practice of astrology, a system of divination using alignments of planets and stars.

**What do you see when you
look at the stars?**

November 24

Ritual is more than just a series of actions. It's a way of being that infuses every aspect of your life with enchantment and possibility. When you embrace ritual, you transform the ordinary into something extraordinary. Whether it's a simple morning routine, a heartfelt gratitude practice, or a sacred ceremony, ritual invites magic to dance in your daily existence.

Through the intentional use of ritual, you can ignite your inner fire, connect with the divine, and manifest your dreams.

November 25

Wisdom is like a guiding light that leads you through life's twists and turns. It's the power to learn from your past, to extract valuable lessons, to make informed choices. In the coming new year let the magic of wisdom guide you towards your highest potential. Embrace the experiences that have shaped you. Combine them with your innate discernment to navigate through life's challenges with grace and clarity.

Wisdom is not just accumulating knowledge; it's about understanding and applying it wisely. It's about using your intuition and insight to make decisions aligned with your true purpose.

November 26

Your magic is not otherworldly. It is very much a part of your humanness. You are given senses and a brain to interpret the universe. You are given consciousness and a body to explore the wonder of you and interact with the wonder around you. Consider your life a work of art, your existence an opportunity for creative magic. Your words and thoughts cast spells. Your actions ripple out from you. Your energy and your will change the world around you.

You are Wild, you are Wise.
You are ready to Rise.

November 27

There are as many paths to power and craft as there are witches to walk them. A thousand doorways stand open to rooms of knowledge and understanding. Let the things that you love guide you to your own unique magic. Follow your passions and your talents and keep yourself open to change and growth. Stay curious. Each moment you are co-creating your life.

Your path is created as you walk it.

November 28

We create habits to survive, and even when we have reached safety or healed our hurts, those habits can be entwined in our lives long after they have served their purpose. To move into thriving may mean releasing old patterns and structure. To thrive will require new ways of doing and being. Don't be afraid and know you have what it takes to live a life beyond survival mode.

Consider what thriving looks like to you and make choices that support your vision.

November 29

Create a sense of comfort around yourself as winter sets in. Whatever makes you feel cozy and cared for should be in your plan for yourself. A thick robe or scented oils. Soft or festive lighting. Blankets, sweaters, delicious hot drinks. And when you are relaxed, let in the dreams that have been at the edge of your life and heart. Let your spirit hold those notions in the coming months, like nature holds life through dark and cold. Spring will come and you will have new things to grow.

**Get quiet enough to hear
your own voice. Create space
to dream and imagine.**

November 30

There's so much as humans that we have discovered about the natural world. From the vastness of space to deep inside our brains, we have explored and learned. And yet there are so many things still to be discovered. Mysteries remain. Your life will not wait for explanations. Your senses are waiting to inform you. Your disciplined, focused mind will aid you. Learn. Know Thyself, because it makes you powerful. Give your energy to what matters.

You are the one you have waited for. Claim your magic.

About The Authors

Terri Clifton is a writer, editor, photographer, and motivational speaker. A triple-threat author, she is published in fiction, non-fiction, and poetry, and awards for her work include a fellowship for emerging fiction literature. She is a life-long advocate for literacy and the importance of the arts in society.

In her free time, she is house photographer for the local historic theatre and teaches writing workshops to all age groups. She is the director of the Chad Clifton Foundation and serves on the Board of Directors for the Calliope Project. She loves travel, nature, live music, and swimming. A part time mermaid who relentlessly pursues Magic in the world and in herself, she continues to study dance and language, and ways to create beauty. She is a believer in thriving, joy, and celebrating life, residing on a historic farm along the Delaware Bay where she raised two boys with her husband, an internationally known wildlife artist.

Bev Adamo is a writer, master life coach, motivational speaker and thought leader. As CEO of Wild & Wise Women, she supports women in discovering their superpowers and living the most fun and meaningful lives possible. She believes in the power of humans to co-create with Source to do the impossible.

In her free time, Bev enjoys an extraordinary relationship with her adult daughter, and has found love again with her husband John. She is a magical rebel in the world, using her unbending intent and willingness to accept the unexpected, and to give hope to all she meets on her daily spiritual walkabout. Enjoying the weather at home in Southern California, Bev also loves to travel, believing in the power of experience to take her deeper into her intuitive, mystical and paradoxical nature.

The Wild and Wise Witch, aka Wild, made herself known during the magical journey Terri and Bev traversed while teaching Magic, living Magic, and writing Magic. Wild has a voice all her own, including the essence of all Women, the Divine Feminine, and the Divine Masculine. Wild is fiercely committed to allow Spirit to move her to bring even more Magic to the world through this book.

Made in the USA
Columbia, SC
22 October 2024